The Lawyer as Leader:

How to Own Your Career and Lead in Law Firms

Author
Antonin Besse

Managing director
Sian O'Neill

The Lawyer as Leader: How to Own Your Career and Lead in Law Firms
is published by

Globe Law and Business Ltd
3 Mylor Close
Horsell
Woking
Surrey GU21 4DD
United Kingdom
Tel: +44 20 3745 4770
www.globelawandbusiness.com

Printed and bound by CPI Group (UK) Ltd, Croydon CR0 4YY, United Kingdom

The Lawyer as Leader: How to Own Your Career and Lead in Law Firms

ISBN 9781787422322
EPUB ISBN 9781787422339
Adobe PDF ISBN 9781787422346
Mobi ISBN 9781787422353

Table of contents

Introduction

This Special Report is about taking control of your career, self-leadership, and leading others in a commercial law firm.

The idea that runs through it is how regaining autonomy and control can transform engagement and fulfilment in a legal career.

I'm a former international commercial lawyer and have worked with lawyers in legal practice and led, coached and developed them for 38 years, 22 as a partner in a Magic Circle firm. This Special Report is eminently practical, based on what I've seen works best, and many things that don't work (including my own mistakes), in the context of successful and fulfilling legal careers and law firm environments. Choice, authorship of your career, and leadership are key themes. The topics are covered from first-hand experience and include:

- leadership;
- building effective teams;
- career planning;
- confidence;
- motivation;
- wellbeing and work–life balance;
- building an internal support network and 'trusted adviser' client relationships;

- communication and feedback;
- project management;
- commerciality; and
- understanding value from the client's perspective.

Commercial law firms are changing and becoming more challenging environments, especially for those who aim to make a career as an equity partner. Knowing what you want, planning your career and carving out your own path are fundamental to success, fulfilment and balance: it's no longer an option simply to think that a partnership would be nice, or to have no stronger guiding principle than, "Let's see what happens". However, the good news is that there are many more career possibilities out there than in the past for lawyers who feel that partnership is not for them, possibly for work–life balance reasons.

Work–life balance, wellbeing and career choice are not new preoccupations. When I was an associate and a partner, you could think about them, but you couldn't really talk about them and you certainly couldn't expect anything to be done about them. While I'm now of an age where I'm thinking more about the carer I want than the career I want, I still think that the profit-driven, competitive commercial law firm partnership remains, deep down, geared towards those who are prepared to sacrifice (almost) everything to business, billings and the bottom line. It's still difficult to admit vulnerability, or to seek and receive regular and open feedback. If things are to change, a new social contract needs to emerge and become part of the zeitgeist. This needs to happen in large part from the bottom up, so it's for associates and the younger partners to understand their choices, say what they think, articulate what they expect, and be clear and forthright into the bargain.

With this in mind, this Special Report is organised as follows:

- chapter I explores the best climate for successful development in a law firm, what makes lawyers tick, and the question of autonomy as the precursor to self-leadership, and leadership more generally;
- chapter II puts forward some ideas about law firms today and future trends as a backdrop to the theme of choice and career fluidity;
- chapter III examines essential leadership skills for commercial lawyers, from communication and business awareness to building effective teams, growing networks and profitable matter management;
- chapter IV looks at self-leadership and proactively shaping the career you want, rather than asking, "What's expected of me?";

- chapter V is an introduction to the coaching skills needed to navigate yourself and others through change in a legal career, with a discussion in chapter VI of those changes that a lawyer is likely to encounter; and
- chapter VII looks at wellbeing.

I. Creating the environment for successful development

1. Inside the lawyer's mind

The law attracts a hugely diverse range of personalities and thinking styles. The variety of challenges, professional environments, subject matters and situations in which lawyers work is equally wide. I can think of few professions like it: the analogy that comes to mind is of a coral reef, where countless aquatic creatures inhabit many specialised ecological niches, each creature exquisitely adapted to its specialism. It is bold, and perhaps foolish, to make an assessment of typical lawyer characteristics – but I shall try.

Lawyers are task-focused: they take instructions, find solutions, get results and serve clients' needs. They like to be right – and they fear getting it wrong, which may be one reason lawyers are often labelled insecure overachievers. Billables loom large over their performance metrics and their perception of value, because that's how they charge for their services. Lawyers tend to specialise, and therefore to be very good at a limited range of tasks. They are analytical, marshalling arguments and taking positions.

What lawyers are not so good at (to some extent the flip side of the characteristics just mentioned) is leadership. It is not the forte of most lawyers I know to take the time to plan and manage matters efficiently, understand value from the client's perspective, be proactive,

"[Lawyers] do not move naturally outside their comfort zone, take risks or experiment in the hope of making serendipitous mistakes, for fear of getting things wrong and being found out."

communicate, listen and give feedback, think outside their silo, and understand and manage people effectively. Lawyers are also, like the White Rabbit in Alice's Wonderland, busily looking at the clock instead of taking time for themselves, asking questions of others, reflecting on their future and taking charge of their careers. They do not move naturally outside their comfort zone, take risks or experiment in the hope of making serendipitous mistakes, for fear of getting things wrong and being found out. This makes it difficult for them to communicate vulnerability and creates a pent-up need for psychological safety, for which law firm environments often fail to cater.

2. Autonomy

Lawyers, particularly partners, enjoy autonomy to a greater degree than most other professions. They guard that autonomy jealously. It is a great source of drive, creativity and empowerment, so the challenge for management in law firms is to nurture it while at the same time ensuring structure, method, collaboration and discipline. All this in a population that considers free agency, and being first among equals, to be an essential part of their identity.

The downside to autonomy is that it can erect strong barriers to behavioural change, financial discipline and effective, joined-up teamwork across departments and offices. The main factors that incentivise lawyers to adopt behaviours that contribute to the greater good of the firm are leadership, trust, reward and threat. Every law firm will rely on a mix of these to keep the partnership cohesive and profitable. In an ideal firm, responsibility lies on the individual to put the client first, the firm second, the team third and themselves last, and to embrace differences and diversity of thought and personality. This is a tall order for humans, who are fundamentally tribal and – in the case of lawyers – very individualistic creatures under pressure to meet ever-tougher performance metrics. So trust suffers, focus on individual financial performance becomes the norm, and the fear factor drives behaviour.

This Special Report will examine how to harness autonomy for good through self-leadership; how to empower others through effective leadership; and how to overcome individualistic tendencies in order to foster motivation, build strong teams, promote collegiality and encourage greater profitability.

These topics will be discussed in more detail below. First, let's look at some of the external pressures shaping law firms and what these will mean for tomorrow's lawyer.

II. Where are commercial law firms heading?

1. The bigger picture

We've highlighted some characteristics of lawyers and sketched law firms as semi-structured collections of autonomously-minded individuals. Before examining these themes in greater detail, we should step back and look at the bigger picture. What are some of the forces that have shaped the modern commercial law firm? What will shape the law firm of tomorrow – in fact, what will its shape be? And how does it all connect with lawyers as human beings, their aspirations, motivations and careers?

2. Money and lateral hires

Remuneration and profitability have long been among the key factors shaping the commercial law firm landscape. The top firms have always regarded what an equity partner takes home as the most important comparative measure of success – more so than size or even clientele. In the UK, Magic Circle partnership earnings were for a long time a close secret, although they were shared confidentially between the top management of those firms. At the same time, in the closing decades of the last century, US law firms were publishing their earnings and profitability, and the level of their top equity partners' earnings seemed, well, magical even to UK Magic Circle partners. Part of the difference lay in the much greater prevalence of the 'eat what you kill' model in US firms, where partners are remunerated largely in line with the business they bring in, as opposed to the more egalitarian 'lockstep' model of UK partnerships, where a partner's share of firm profits depends on seniority.

The first two decades of this century have seen a very rapid – and accelerating – evolution of partner and, to a lesser extent, associate remuneration in London firms. The reason that partner remuneration was, and continues to be, regarded as such a key metric is perversely Darwinian: the richest partners could recruit the best talent, thereby enhancing their reputation and in turn attracting the top clients and the largest deals. Why the largest deals? Simply because those tend to be the life or death (or 'bet the farm') events in corporate life, such as contested takeovers and global investigations, with existential implications, where hiring anything less than the best advisory talent is not an option. As the US firms began to set up in Europe, especially London, in increasing numbers, they began to hire local talent by offering attractive remuneration packages. This led to UK firms modifying their remuneration models – sometimes in an awkwardly *ad hoc* fashion in the case of the lockstep firms – first to protect themselves from the prospect of their best partners being poached, and second to be able to poach their own lateral hires.

The knock-on effects on law firm culture and structure in the top firms have been considerable.

"The rise of the lateral hire has dislocated law firm collegiality by replacing the notion of partnership for life with the ideas that partners are, at the successful end of the scale, highly remunerated hired guns, and at the less successful end, struggling individuals on metrics-driven tenure."

The rise of the lateral hire has dislocated law firm collegiality by replacing the notion of partnership for life with the ideas that partners are, at the successful end of the scale, highly remunerated hired guns, and at the less successful end, struggling individuals on metrics-driven tenure.

There has also been another phenomenon which I call 'equity book-ending'. The most important measure of law firm profitability – and therefore of success – is profit per equity partner. That has led to a shrinking of the number of equity partners in law firms relative to the total number of partners, with non-equity partners being remunerated very much like salaried associates. It is now not only more difficult to become an equity partner, as the available slots are limited, but associates have to wait longer (until their mid- to late thirties) to step up to equity. They are then under increasing pressure to step down from equity when they reach their fifties to make room for the younger generation. This trend has accelerated because of demographics, as the baby boomers are now in their fifties and early sixties. So equity is a prize available to fewer, later and for a shorter period of time. This equity book-ending boosts profit per equity partner, but puts greater pressures on work–life balance. It therefore makes the question, "Do I want to be a partner?" starker and more relevant than ever. What alternatives are there? And should lawyers prepare for a second career? These questions are dealt with in chapters IV and VI below.

3. Globalisation and mergers

Two other important factors driving the size and shape of commercial law firms have been globalisation and mergers.

The globalisation of business has led many firms to position themselves as world or, at the very least, international players with a ubiquitous ability to service clients' needs. There are many ways to do this credibly, with the approaches falling into three categories, as follows.

Three approaches to global positioning

- The 'best friends' approach – team up with trusted independent partner firms in other countries and cement the partnership with such things as exclusive referral, secondment and training arrangements.
- The 'buy or grow your own' approach – merge with firms in other jurisdictions, or found offices from scratch by hiring local lawyers.
- An *ad hoc* combination of the first two approaches – a best friends strategy for some jurisdictions and a local presence in others.

While the first approach requires the least investment, and is therefore less dilutive of profits, it offers the least control over quality and the ability to offer a single brand and way of doing things across jurisdictions. On the other hand, it enables close links with the best local firms and the opportunity to tap into their reputation and client base. It is also flexible. The second approach theoretically offers the ability to offer a single global brand and one stop shop to clients, and to project as a large international player with lots of lawyers and vast geographic reach. The reality is sometimes a bit different: local hires are not always the best local players, and getting lawyers to work seamlessly and to single standards of quality across jurisdictions is not always easy, for the reasons examined in chapter III, section 8, "Working effectively across borders".

Mergers have also characterised the commercial law firm scene in the past thirty years or so, both nationally and internationally. This has been partly driven by globalisation, but also by a perceived competitive need to grow a strong brand, combine resources, increase reach and swell the bottom line in order to succeed and survive. Many firms have buckled under economic pressure and poor management and have been taken over. While some firms coming out of these multiple mergers have thrived – largely through excellent leadership – others have not, struggling to reconcile different cultures, DNAs, working methods and systems. The reasons for successful or unsuccessful integration are touched upon in chapter VI, section 1.6, "Integrating new teams and mergers".

4. Now, and then what?

The past ten years have seen a large number of other changes in the shape and direction of commercial law firms, driven by tech, profitability and, for want of a better term, fragmentation of the workforce. We shall look at some of those changes, and speculate about what the future might hold.

4.1 Technology

Technology is a huge subject, so I'll just pull out some strands and look at them briefly.

Tech in the legal services industry

- First, tech is partly riding, partly driving the trend to outsource low-cost volume and repetitive work either to artificial intelligence systems such as due diligence tools or dedicated legal service centres located elsewhere, with the aim of lowering infrastructure and labour costs. This is taking quite a big chunk out of trainees' and junior lawyers' traditional diet of work and theoretically freeing them up to do more high-value work.

- Secondly, tech is changing the way we communicate and work together: millennials use email less readily, preferring social media and flexible, multipurpose communication and collaboration tools such as Slack. The consequences of this change have not yet revolutionised workplace communications but they will, as succeeding generations follow the millennials.
- Thirdly, there has been something of a scramble to embrace technological change, which has given rise to some interesting experiments. Two that I find striking are that many law firms have founded tech and fintech start-up incubators, and that some law firms are training their lawyers to code. Well, why not? Some may see these initiatives as bold experiments that could pay off handsomely. Others may dismiss them as PR initiatives to burnish the 21st-century image of the law firms involved. I see them as a welcome and inevitable trend towards the hybridisation of the legal services industry, one of the spinoffs of which will be increased career choice.

4.2 Hybridisation

Hybridisation is already taking many forms. Legal services centres and tech specialists play an increasingly important role in law firms, as do other forms of business support service. These include pricing and project managers, business development specialists and knowledge managers, who may have no legal experience and work alongside lawyers in a client-facing capacity or in C-suite roles.

4.3 The lawyer as management consultant

The hybridisation of the law firm population by the introduction of these specialists is driven by competition, and in particular the need to bring down the cost of producing legal services. They help to provide better value to the client and speak the language that clients understand, particularly when it comes to fee negotiations (see chapter III, section 6, "Business awareness"). The focus on client value has also led to an increasing realisation that many clients are not just looking for legal solutions to their problems – they want solutions, full stop. Much more emphasis is being put on getting lawyers to think commercially; in fact to think first about the business issues before focusing on the legal issues, and to think more like management consultants.

4.4 Scrapping the juniors and training

The lateral hiring trend, fuelled by remuneration competition at both partner and associate level, is combining with pricing pressures driven by large clients to have a nefarious effect on training. The difficulty is that because of the fluidity of the legal employment market, many associates are being hired ready-trained at high salaries, while many large clients simply refuse to pay for trainee and junior lawyers' work.

"[I]t may be that global professional service superfirms will emerge in the future combining lawyers with accountants, management consultants and possibly even investment bankers."

These market forces could converge to reduce investment in hiring and training junior lawyers, and indeed there are signs that this is the case already. At the same time, lawyers are being required to deploy an expanded range of skills earlier in their careers, particularly interpersonal and client-facing skills, commercial thinking, and understanding value from the client's perspective.

4.5 Contract working and the demise of the hierarchy

The contract lawyer and flexible law firm phenomenon, which has grown in recent years, ticks many boxes. Truly flexible working arrangements are a holy grail for many lawyers seeking to escape a constant diet of gruelling hours and a sterile personal life, either temporary (caring for family, whether young or old, for example) or permanent (because they wish to pursue other opportunities in parallel). In addition, they provide a ready-trained and trusted source of legal talent for firms and in-house legal departments who avoid the fixed overheads associated with having lawyers on their books as employees. Above all, the notion of flexible working is perfectly in tune with today's labour economy and the increasing emphasis that those at the younger end of the workforce are placing on choice and work–life balance. It is possible to imagine a not-so-distant future where it is normal for large deals, investigations and pieces of litigation to be dealt with by independent specialists who come together for the purpose of executing a particular project. I would also speculate that that the appetite of millennials for more flexible, less hierarchical, working environments will blur the lines between employees and contract workers in the legal industry to a far greater extent than today. That change may be catalysed by the shifts in ownership structures discussed below.

4.6 New ownership structures

Not so long ago, partner ownership of law firms was the only game in town: the partners of a firm held the equity, owned the capital, reaped the profits and bore the risks of the business. New ownership models have now emerged and are taking hold: private equity investment and IPOs, for example, are shifting ownership and the locus of economic control away from partners into the hands of investors and shareholders. The allocation of risks, rewards and incentives are changing radically. I would argue that one of the consequences is that the distinction between associate and partner will disappear and that this may allow firms to become more flexible and creative in rewarding different categories of lawyers with different career ambitions. Changes in ownership structures and the reallocation of risk and reward also go hand in hand with many other changes discussed in this chapter, including the growth of contract working and the flattening of hierarchy, the hybridisation of firms, the creation of superfirms and investment in start-ups.

4.7 Superfirms

Much is being said today about what clients expect their law firms to bring them, including solutions to business, not just legal, problems as mentioned above. There are certainly some who believe that lawyers must be trained to think with a business mindset first, and it may be that global professional service superfirms will emerge in the future combining lawyers with accountants, management consultants and possibly even investment bankers. Those firms will probably no longer price their services by the hour, but by the added value they generate. Whatever the future of the commercial legal profession, it is undoubtedly true that the commercial lawyer of today needs a strong grasp of commerciality and an understanding of clients' businesses, as well as what value means to clients. How this can be achieved is examined in chapter III, section 7, "Managing deals for value".

"Law firms do not promote or buy in partner talent primarily for their leadership skills, but rather for their rain-making abilities. So law firms are not natural incubators of good leaders."

III. Lawyers as leaders

1. Introduction

Tetsuro Matsuzawa has been studying chimpanzees for many years, and has observed that their short-term memory far surpasses that of humans. When presented briefly with several numbers placed randomly around a screen, they can remember exactly where those numbers were, in numerical order. And they can do this after being allowed to look at the numbers for only half a second. Very few humans can do this. Given that chimpanzees have very similar brains to ours, what explains the difference in short-term memory skills? One theory is that humans developed imagination – the ability to visualise events in the past and in the future, and to think strategically using that ability – as well as language, enabling us to communicate that imagination, and to develop a survival strategy based on the sharing of ideas and cooperation, but at the expense of short-term memory.

The story offers an interesting hypothesis for the origin of an ability which lies at the heart of good leadership: to formulate ideas and transmit them in a way that engenders cooperation. How effective leaders do this, and how effective cooperation happens in teams, is the subject of this chapter. A key theme is good communication through listening.

2. Leaders or rainmakers?

Lawyers are not well trained as leaders. Lawyers are above all task-oriented, and are at their best when acting on instructions. When associates turn their minds to their careers, their first reaction is often to ask, "What's expected of me?" rather than, "What drives, me, and where do I want to go?". Law firms do not promote or buy in partner talent primarily for their leadership skills, but rather for their rain-making abilities. So law firms are not natural incubators of good leaders.

2.1 The good leader

Command is: Wisdom, Integrity, Compassion, Courage, Severity.
Sun Tzu, *The Art of War*.[1]

This quote from Sun Tzu is not an exhaustive enumeration of good leadership attributes. But it is a helpful start. The next few paragraphs look at some of these attributes, as well as others, in more detail. What follows is necessarily selective, given that leadership is a vast subject. My selection is governed by what I consider to be the most important leadership characteristics for lawyers.

A good leader has clear goals: a vision of what they want to achieve with, and for, others. This vision is founded on a sense of purpose

"Good leaders know their value to others and understand the goals, values and drivers of others thanks to empathy and communication – questioning, listening and challenging."

based on values and drivers. Understanding them requires self-appraisal and self-awareness. Good leaders know their value to others and understand the goals, values and drivers of others thanks to empathy and communication – questioning, listening and challenging. Good leaders will open themselves to challenge, and hold themselves to account, by actively seeking feedback. They will communicate their vision by sharing, adapting and adjusting it to integrate the views and aspirations of others, thereby fostering a sense of co-creation and partnership which in turn engenders trust and cooperation. They will empower and facilitate; they will not wield power. There are no leaders without followers. Leaders need to inspire and enable those followers and tap into people's natural desires to believe in unifying ideas, myths and stories. Without that desire we wouldn't have laws, political systems, money or religion.[2]

2.2 Self-appraisal

Know the enemy, know yourself, and victory is never in doubt, not in a hundred battles.
Sun Tzu, *The Art of War*.[3]

The importance of self-awareness is a recurring theme of this Special Report, and is discussed in detail in chapter V. Clarity of purpose and goals are essential in any leader, but equally important is clarity about the style of leadership that suits that leader.

A good leader will score highly on other aspects of emotional intelligence: the ability to read others' feelings and motives and create connections with, and between, people. Emotional intelligence is discussed in chapter V.

How a leader chooses to lead will be informed by personal experience of good and poor leadership; those experiences are well worth writing down as part of any leader's self-appraisal. My guiding principle is: Be the leader that you want to be led by. A sample tool to help you think about your leadership style can be found in Appendix 1.

2.3 Inspiring others

Without knowing the plans of the feudal lords, you cannot form alliances. Without knowing the lie of hills and woods, of cliffs and crags, of marshes and fens, you cannot march. Without using local guides, you cannot exploit the lie of the land.
Sun Tzu, *The Art of War*.[4]

Leadership requires an understanding of what others want, and a willingness to adapt one's objectives and designs to those of others. It is the only way to gain trust and cooperation. That understanding comes about through communicating those designs, being honest and transparent in doing so, soliciting feedback, listening, and making others feel as if they are being heard – see section 4 of this chapter, "Communication, feedback and critical conversations". The cycle should be repeated regularly. Appealing to autonomy and people's potential is an important part of this process. Managing people by rules and diktat will not inspire, whereas suggesting, reflecting and listening will. I remember a particularly effective senior partner who would make his partners feel valued by regularly soliciting their views, and giving the impression of really listening: a rare thing in a large law firm. It feels easier to accept, and more rewarding to implement, goals and purposes in which you have been given a say.

Good leaders show integrity and lack of self-interest, and lead by example – they set standards for others to follow. The charismatic leader will inspire through enthusiasm and even awe, and by gaining respect through behaviour that goes above and beyond. An inspiring leader is authentic: the strength of his or her core values and beliefs will communicate themselves through goals, purpose, vision and behaviour as well as words.

Leading by example means leading visibly. Making people feel valued means investing time with them and really paying attention. Emails and texts don't create relationships; walking and talking do. Sharing purpose and vision means telling stories. Setting standards means calling out bad behaviour immediately, and ringing the bell for good behaviour.

2.4 Leading through change and uncertainty

People are always looking to leaders (more precisely, good leaders) in uncertain times. Natural leaders are attuned to, and energised by, the needs that others have for leadership, and will meet those needs by stepping forward with initiatives. For those of us who do not count ourselves natural leaders, it's worth noting that we all take our cues from each other. So in that sense everyone leads and exercises influence by communicating, listening and doing.

What people also want in times of change is information and transparency – they want to know what's going to happen, and they want to be able to assess threats and opportunities that might be brought about by the change. They also want to feel that they have some measure of control by having a say and being heard. For all these reasons, a good leader will share the plan for change, give people a say, listen to feedback and where possible adapt the plan accordingly. It is more important for people to feel that they are heard and understood, than for them to see all of their views reflected in a plan. Particularly when there is resistance to change, a good leader will accomplish much by simply soliciting people individually and asking them, "What would help to get you on board?". Asking the question, acknowledging the answer and showing empathy is often sufficient to gain an ally.

SMART goals

Creating disciples and champions for any change within an organisation is important, as is setting and communicating SMART goals. Goals should be:

- Specific
- Measurable
- Action-based
- Realistic
- Time-based

What is measurable gets done.

Above all, particularly in times of change, by creating a sense of shared purpose and an environment in which people feel understood, valued and empowered, a good leader will make people feel safe. Creating a sense of psychological safety in law firms whose members tend to be insecure overachievers is absolutely key (for more on this see chapter VII, section 4, "Fear and loathing in law firms – a plea for psychological safety").

3. Effective legal teams

3.1 What lawyers don't do well

In all my years as a transaction lawyer, it was an all-too-rare pleasure to work in a team that operated seamlessly across groups, departments and offices. What I noticed was that lawyers are never happier than when doing something they are good at with the small number of people they know and trust. The role of the other players in the transaction, either in the their own firm or outside, is at best part of their peripheral vision, not a central concern. I have been involved in major cross-border restructurings where tax lawyers, crucial to the transaction, were only brought in at the last minute. The basic questions that need to be asked at the beginning of the transaction, including, "Who needs to be involved, or at least given a heads up about this?", are often not asked. The group receiving the instructions will happily run with the deal, doing what they do well, until a fair way down the line the realisation sinks in that other pools of expertise must be brought in. Summoning them late to a hot and busy kitchen with very little lead time gives them the impression that their contribution is secondary, that they are being dictated to and treated like inferiors, and their commitment suffers accordingly. In short, this is a failure of leadership, planning and communication, all key ingredients of good teamwork which we'll look at in the following paragraphs.

3.2 What makes a good team?

An effective team has an identity. The team members feel that they belong to it through shared goals, a shared sense of purpose and a sense of co-creation. These things are built through leadership and consensus, the two inextricably linked since a good part of effective leadership lies in bringing about consensus and buy-in. A good team will be clear about what good looks like – what qualitative and quantitative targets need to be met, and the deadlines for meeting these. Hallmarks of effective teams are:

- mutual accountability;
- taking responsibility for others;
- an understanding on the part of each team member that the team depends on their individual contribution;
- a willingness to ring the bell for good behaviour, with an emphasis on collective success;
- a commitment to challenge and call out bad behaviour; and
- recording commitments and achievement.

Understanding and respecting differences in skills, personalities and styles of behaviour in a team is also very important. A great team will tap into individual talents to create something that is more than the sum of its parts, and do so in a way that empowers each team member by giving them a sense that they are being respected and valued for their individuality. Similarly, a good team leader will leverage the strengths of other team members to overcome weaknesses.

The best teams will, at an early stage in the team's formation, get three things clear:

- what value each team member brings to the team – this helps define their role;
- what each team member values about being part of the team – this identifies their motivation; and
- what support each team member expects to receive from the other team members – this creates shared purpose and accountability.

The other things that should be discussed and agreed at an early stage are:

- the team's objectives (in the form of SMART goals);
- basic values;
- members' roles;
- how and when the team will communicate and meet;
- a commitment to listen, challenge and hold each other to account; and
- how the team will be led.

"Accountability for behaviour, contributions, standards and values will always lead to good discipline and high performance."

In discussing and agreeing those things, it's helpful if each team member can share a story about a good team experience and a bad team experience from their past.

Accountability for behaviour, contributions, standards and values will always lead to good discipline and high performance. That is why team meetings to review progress and call in commitments are key. They give team members an opportunity to hold each other to account in a respectful listening environment (see section 4.3 of this chapter, "Successful meetings"). Adjustments to goals and the way the team functions can then be agreed based on a review of performance to date.

3.3 The Five Dysfunctions of a Team

Patrick Lencioni has written extensively on the behaviour that makes for good teamwork, and is best known for his Five Dysfunctions of a Team model illustrated in Figure 1 below. This emphasises that absence of trust and fear of conflict, which come about through poor communication and lack of transparency and accountability, make for a dysfunctional team.

Figure 1: Lencioni's Five Dysfunctions of a Team

Starting from the bottom of the pyramid, the five dysfunctions are:[5]

1. *Absence of trust:* Fear of being vulnerable and open with team members gets in the way of building trust.
2. *Fear of conflict:* Issues don't get aired and debated honestly and constructively.
3. *Lack of commitment:* Lack of clarity or buy-in prevents the making of decisions that people will stick to.
4. *Avoidance of accountability:* Team members don't call out bad behaviour or poor performance.
5. *Inattention to results:* Individualistic behaviour erodes focus on collective success.

Team members in successful teams:

- are comfortable with asking for support, ringing the bell for each other, admitting that they are wrong, and offering and receiving feedback;
- know what each team member has to offer, and tap into the skills and experience of the other team members;
- avoid the same issues being repeatedly brought up because of lack of discussion and acceptance by the other members of the team;
- raise difficult or important issues and have energetic, open and respectful debates about them; and
- ensure that the team members share the same goals and point in the same direction.

4. Communication, feedback and critical conversations

4.1 Communication

Perhaps because law firms are made up of autonomous, task- and target-focused individuals, communication is not their strong point. In addition, lawyers are reluctant to share personal issues in troubled times because, quite simply, vulnerability is perceived as weakness. On the other hand, a law firm culture that encourages communication and feedback can bring huge benefits.

Lawyers who communicate well with others at the start of, and throughout, a matter will create a sense of equality, partnership and buy-in, which in turn engenders trust and collegiality. As mentioned above, what so often happens is that colleagues in other departments and offices are instructed at the last minute or well after the matter has got under way. This signals poor planning, a lack of respect and a feeling by colleagues that they are being treated as second-class citizens.

Regular communication with clients, if only on cost reporting, manages expectations and shows transparency and good project management skills, thereby earning client trust. More often than not, what happens instead is that lawyers wait until the end of a matter to

"Lawyers who communicate well with others at the start of, and throughout, a matter will create a sense of equality, partnership and buy-in, which in turn engenders trust and collegiality."

raise cost overruns with the client, which will inevitably raise hackles and lead to damaged client relations and the erosion of profits through write-offs (see section 7.1 of this chapter, "What is legal project management?").

4.2 Feedback

Feedback is usually something that happens once a year in the context of a somewhat bureaucratic annual appraisal process, possibly accompanied by a 360° exercise. It is rare for partners to give regular unsolicited feedback to associates, and even rarer for associates to ask for it. It is rarer still for feedback to be given between partners. Downward feedback to trainees and junior associates is often poorly handled: a busy associate or partner might prefer to rewrite a junior's work themselves than to go through the time-consuming task of sitting down with the junior, working through the draft with constructive criticism, and getting them to redraft it in the knowledge that it may require a second or third round of review and constructive criticism before it can be sent to the partner or client. This disempowers and demotivates the junior, and deprives the senior of an opportunity to pass on valuable lessons.

Lack of proper feedback, either about career direction or specific tasks, leaves lawyers, who are naturally under-confident overachievers, feeling unfulfilled and undervalued. This is an especially strident complaint amongst millennials, who are more focused on work–life balance issues and whose sense of loyalty to employers is looser than that of previous generations. They value responsibility and they want to feel that people take an interest in them. Failure to recognise this harms talent retention, and employer reputation can suffer instantly online, through social media and otherwise.

Post-transaction reviews, both internal and with the client, are often ignored or botched because lawyers dread receiving criticism. And yet regular, honest feedback sessions with clients are critical to building client trust and loyalty. We look at this in greater detail below, in section 7, "Managing deals for value".

So what does good feedback look like? The answer will become clear in the following paragraphs which deal with listening and effective communication.

4.3 Successful meetings

Good communication, and therefore good leadership, is founded on listening. Anyone who has experienced it will understand the benefit of simply being listened to for understanding. Listening for understanding is an aim in itself, and not a means or prelude for imposing a point of view.

The listening environment

In an ideal world, every lawyer would be familiar with Nancy Kline's listening environment as described in her 2002 book, *Time to Think: Listening to Ignite the Human Mind*.[6] She sets out an effective way to conduct meetings in a manner that not only gives everyone an equal say, but also ensures that those who have a tendency to remain silent and internalise their frustrations, often to the detriment of team morale and performance, speak their mind. To conduct a successful meeting using this method, the leader or chair will:

- first go round the table, ensuring that everyone has a turn to speak without interruption;
- ask each person to start by saying what is going well;
- ask open questions to remove limiting assumptions (eg, "What's stopping you?" or "If you had a magic wand, what might you do to solve this issue?");
- summarise;
- go around each participant a second time; and
- summarise and set out agreed actions.

This is a very effective way to create buy-in and commitment in a team by giving each person that feeling that they are being heard and understood, and accepted and respected as an equal partner in the team. For a leader, it is a helpful method for reading the room, or checking on the mood of the group and attuning to that mood by summarising and playing back what has been said.

4.4 Effective client conversations

Walking a mile in the other person's shoes is a leadership habit that lawyers can usefully learn. One area where this is particularly obvious is business development. Lawyers will instinctively tell the client how good and how well suited they are to handling the client's business. Clients, on the other hand, would generally prefer to be asked knowledgeable questions by an interested listener about their business and the issues they face. Having lawyers conduct role plays to rehearse critical client conversations can be invaluable. A useful tool in this context is the 'perceptual positions' exercise described in chapter V, section 8, "Walking in another's shoes".

4.5 Difficult conversations, and calling out bad behaviour

There is a tendency to think that others can't change and that whatever one says or does will have zero impact, especially in the upper echelons of an organisation. People don't like saying what they think out of risk-aversion, fear of being wrong, telling their boss what they don't want to hear or being criticised themselves. That leads to passivity, the internalisation of problems and the consequent sapping of morale.

"The ability to conduct effective listening conversations in which both parties feel that their point of view is being heard and valued, rather than feel threatened, is an easy skill to learn."

As we've seen, a good leader will instil a habit of regular feedback conversations where difficult issues are aired honestly and respectfully and where everyone in the organisation is encouraged to call out bad behaviour and hold others – and for that matter themselves – to account.

Conducting a 'difficult' feedback conversation

- What do I want from this conversation? The first thing in any feedback conversation is to visualise a clear outcome: what will a successful conversation look like?
- Identify the issue and avoid making it personal. The next thing is to work out how to bring up the difficult issue. The art here is to depersonalise the conversation by identifying the issue or the behaviour clearly, and describing the effect it has had on the speaker. This will avoid the other person feeling accused by shifting the focus to the effect of their actions on others as opposed to characterising the actions themselves (eg, "What you did made me feel bad about myself" is less accusatory than, "What you did shows that you're a callous and selfish person"). It is also helpful at the outset to agree that each party will have a set time – three minutes, say – to express themselves uninterrupted by the other, and then to switch

over so that everyone feels that they are being afforded equal treatment and respect.
- Give examples. It is important to give examples to anchor what one says: "When that happened, I thought X" or "When that happened, I felt Y". Focusing on the behaviour and the effect of that behaviour, rather than the perpetrator, preserves respect and minimises loss of self-esteem.
- Commitment to action. At the conclusion of the conversation, each party should undertake action to improve matters, if only by agreeing a date to meet again to discuss progress.

The ability to conduct effective listening conversations in which both parties feel that their point of view is being heard and valued, rather than feel threatened, is an easy skill to learn. It will lead to feedback becoming routine rather than something that has to happen formulaically once a year, or at the end of a matter, or that is to be avoided altogether. Armed with this skill, lawyers can transform their environment into one where trust, collegiality and accountability become the norm.

5. Building your connections

Taking the initiative and building connections are two hallmarks of successful leaders. But why is getting out there, knocking on doors, telling the world about yourself, making connections and building relationships so important?

5.1 Support

The first part of the answer lies in the question, "How many calls would you need to make to get another job?" I was recently told about the CFO of a FTSE 100 company who received several networking approaches a day until the time when he was made redundant because of a downturn. In the following weeks he received only one call from one of his former contacts, a lawyer, asking how he was. Several months later he got a new position as CFO in a large multinational. He never forgot that one caller, and soon put a large matter her way.

Your support network, both personal and professional, is the one asset that will always follow you from job to job, from country to country, from one set of personal circumstances to the next. It has been compared to savings or a pension: if you pay into it in the good times by making the effort to cultivate connections (more about that later), you can draw on it in times of need.

As we've already seen, building support is an integral part of leadership, teamwork and communication. It involves making personal connections – making others feel valued by investing time and effort in them on a regular basis, and even in difficult times, as the story about the CFO illustrates.

To connect with people, you need have no other excuse than sharing a background, experience or interest, professional or otherwise. In some cases the connection can be made with a view to a particular shared objective (for example when enlisting the support of a champion for a partnership candidacy – see chapter IV, section 4, "What does it take to make partner?"), or for the purpose of an arrangement which is mutually beneficial. The key is that the connection should be based on some commonality, something that both parties can identify with, something that appeals to the collaborative, social, tribal animals we are.

5.2 Visibility

Another reason for making connections is visibility: getting others to understand who you are and what you do. Lawyers tend not to do this so well, and yet managing your brand and profile – your area of expertise and what you stand for – and making sure that others know about it is crucial, both internally within the firm and externally in the market. Without recognition and visibility, no senior associate will make partner, and no partner will build a practice.

Much of what it takes to build visibility lies in planning your career, knowing your value proposition, and advancing your career goals as discussed below. This requires knowing where you're going and what you want to be known for, and building relationships with others both inside and outside the firm to make it happen.

5.3 Business development

The reaction I get most often when talking about business development to lawyers is a mixture of squeamishness at selling themselves and awkwardness about how to engage with others. Networking brings to mind stilted conversations at drinks and canapé functions and forced conversations at industry conferences. The fear of rejection and humiliation lurks close to the surface and, for some, the phobia of being 'found out' plays its part as well (see chapter V, section 12.4, "Impostor syndrome" for a discussion of this topic).

In reality, clients expect to be on the receiving end of business development initiatives. They like feeling cared for, valued, being made to feel special, and they want information, leads and contacts that will advance their careers or support their business. That doesn't mean inviting them once in a blue moon to a go-karting event (although some clients do enjoy go-karting); it means a personal touch – sending them information and articles of interest with an "I thought of you when I came across this" message, calling them for a chat about it and sharing a bit of market intelligence. It means inviting them to special events that you know they will enjoy (because you know they love Ed Sheeran, or cosplay, or the ballet), or introducing them to contacts who will be valuable to them. It means knowing about their family. It means following up on transactions and asking for their feedback. It means knowing whether they like dogs or cats, or keep a pet tarantula. It means asking questions about clients as individuals, their business and their preoccupations: what is a concern for them right now? It means doing this regularly. It means being generous with your time and energy, and not expecting an immediate return on investment.

5.4 Networking conversations

An effective networking conversation will always have a dual goal.

- What do I want to find out about this person, and what questions should I ask to do this?
- What outcome would I like to achieve? This could be another meeting, an introduction, a lunch, anything that will keep the relationship going and bring some value to you and preferably the other person as well.

To take the sting out of networking conversations, it is best to approach them not as an occasion where you have to sell yourself, but rather as an opportunity to get the other person to talk about themselves. Ask open questions of the "What do you enjoy about

"[Networking] means asking questions about clients as individuals, their business and their preoccupations: what is a concern for them right now? It means doing this regularly. It means being generous with your time and energy, and not expecting an immediate return on investment."

your job?" or "What's your organisation's main challenge?" variety. People are generally more comfortable answering questions and talking about themselves than listening to someone talking at them in full sales mode. Listen – really listen to them, be fully present, mirror their body language and reflect their words back. To quote some excellent advice from Olivia Fox Cabane, who has written extensively on charisma: "Don't try to impress them. Let them impress you. They will love you for it."[7]

5.5 Planning and executing a networking strategy

The best networking is planned. You need to know who you want to cultivate for the purposes of your career goals, and have a time-based plan for approaching them and building a relationship. It is also important, when fixing networking objectives, to be clear about what success will look like. The career planning template in Appendix 2 contains a sample client plan with some examples of this.

It may be helpful, when executing your plan, to keep a chart recording who you have contacted and when; their organisation; very brief information on the last contact; and a deadline for follow-up action. This is something that can be delegated to a PA or EA, who can be tasked with holding you to account on the follow-up.

"Don't try to impress them. Let them impress you. They will love you for it."

Olivia Fox Cabane

Key factors in successful networking are:

- planning;
- persistence;
- follow-up;
- regularity; and
- patience.

When you plant a garden, not all the plants will thrive, and others will take time to grow. You will also need to talk to them and make them feel loved.

5.6 The *consigliere*: becoming a trusted adviser

The ingredients of trust

Before leaving the subject of networking, I will touch briefly on an equation originally made famous by David Maister in *The Trusted Advisor*.[8] It represents a bold and enlightening attempt at reducing the ingredients in effective business relationships to a formula:

$$\text{Trust} = \frac{\text{Credibility} + \text{Reliability} + \text{Intimacy}}{\text{Self-interest}}$$

The idea behind the formula is that strong adviser/client *consigliere*-type relationships are based on trust, and that trust is made up of:

- Credibility. This is based on a number of factors including experience, confidence and gravitas, and answers the questions, "Is this person capable of doing what I need them to do? Will they make me look good? Will they be able to save my organisation from flame and ruin in a crisis?"
- Reliability. Does your track record prove that you will do what you say you can do? That is, will you walk the walk and execute on time and on budget?
- Intimacy. This means building a personal connection as discussed in section 5.3 above, such that the client feels that you value, understand and care for them as a person (personal intimacy) and that you also understand their business and organisation (business intimacy).
- Self-interest. This means the degree to which you are in it for yourself, and whether your motive for building a relationship is purely selfish. As the denominator of the equation, the more self-interest the client perceives you to have in building the relationship, the more the trust built up by the combination of credibility, reliability and intimacy will be diminished. Self-interest dilutes and weakens trust.

I heard a telling anecdote from a law firm partner, Henry, which says something about intimacy as well as self-interest. On the day of the Brexit referendum result in 2016, in the numbed silence that descended on the City, a senior banker sat at his desk. He was painfully processing the events and wondering about the uncertain future that came with them. Henry called him in the afternoon and asked how he was and how he felt. Nothing more. Just how he was, and how he felt. The client was clearly relieved to be able to share his woes, adding that not one of his other advisers had made contact. He will remember that call, and he will remember Henry.

6. Business awareness

6.1 What's driving the client?

The short answer is: value for money. The way fees are negotiated between law firms and large clients, and those clients' fee expectations, have changed radically over the past few years. The traditional annual discussions between senior client partners and general counsel have in many cases been replaced by more soulless, hard-driven discussions around pricing led by client procurement departments. Bills are sent out by those clients for auditing by specialist consultants who are paid a percentage of the savings that they manage to obtain. Some clients no longer want to pay for juniors; impose a cap on the number of lawyers at meetings; require 'matriculation freezes' (meaning that lawyers who start work on a matter are always charged at the same rate throughout the matter without any increase reflecting advances in seniority, even if the matter takes years); and refuse to allow more than a certain number of hours per lawyer to be billed. These are the sorts of client expectations and pressures that are driving the creation of legal services centres, lawyer-on-demand hubs, and efficiencies through AI and the professionalisation of the project management and pricing functions in law firms.

6.2 The chargeable hour: time for change

But there is a factor lagging behind these modernisation initiatives, and that is the lawyer's mindset on value and matter management. We'll look at value mindset here; matter management is dealt with in sections 7 and 8 below.

A lawyer's notion of value is based on the chargeable hour. This is still largely the unit of measurement of key internal performance metrics such as total hours, utilisation and realisations. These are used for purposes of pay, bonuses and promotion. The chargeable hour is also the key unit for measuring the cost, and therefore – in the eyes of most lawyers – the value of a day's work.

But does the client see it that way? How does the client perceive the value of that day's work? What does value mean to a particular client in the context of a particular matter? These are the questions that lawyers should be asking at the outset, and they should build their fee proposals accordingly. This is where a commercial approach pays – understanding the client's business, and asking the right questions of the client, will achieve alignment of thinking and creative fee deals, such as percentage-of-value success fees and innovative risk-sharing and co-investment fee structures.

6.3 Profitability: what associates need to know

Associates rarely get involved in formulating fee deals and negotiating price. They may get some exposure to this as senior associates, although the tendency is to think that this sort of thing is very much in the partners' domain.

This doesn't prepare lawyers well for their transition to partnership. From their first day as partners, for every £100,000 of equity profit, they will need to generate approximately £200,000 in fees, year in, year out, to maintain the margins that top firms are used to. In firms where junior partners take home upwards of £1,000,000, a new partner will need to generate at least £2,000,000 in fees in their first year.

"[U]nderstanding the client's business, and asking the right questions of the client, will achieve alignment of thinking and creative fee deals, such as percentage-of-value success fees and innovative risk-sharing and co-investment fee structures."

7. Managing deals for value

What would you do to improve your firm's bottom line by 10%? The answer is easier than you might think, and much of it lies in better project management. Of the gross fees a firm generates, anything between 15% and 20%, sometimes more, gets written off. Something around a third of that tends to be down to poor transaction management. Examples include inaccurate price quotes because a matter has not been adequately scoped and priced, out-of-scope work not being discussed and authorised with the client, poor time and cost recording, poor communication and inadequate fee reporting.

7.1 What is legal project management?

The essentials of project management, which are contained in the Plan, Do, Check and Review cycle illustrated below, are applicable to any task, large or small. It's a frame of mind, a way of thinking about how you do things and coordinate with others involved in the task or project. As we've already seen, lawyers are good at doing, and not so good at planning. As solution- and task-focused beings, they want to get the job done (which they can charge for) and will tend to skimp on, or skip altogether, the planning and scoping stage, for which they believe they can't charge. Nor are they good at thinking outside of their silos, that is, coordinating early on with the other players in the project, and keeping information about the project flowing among those players during the execution phase.

The Plan, Do, Check and Review cycle

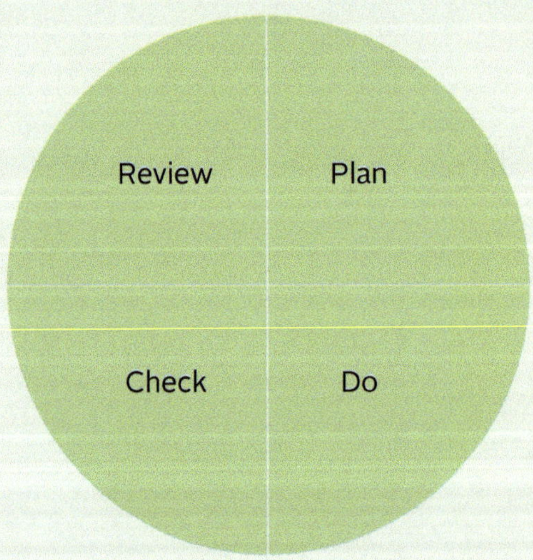

In a legal project, the cycle means delivering quality and efficiency by focusing on:

- *Planning:* Proper scoping; scheduling and resourcing; and pricing.
- *Doing and Checking:* Monitoring and communicating; and adapting scope, schedule, resourcing and pricing to new events or changes of plan.
- *Reviewing:* Learning lessons internally and with the client, and applying them not only at the end but throughout the matter, and subsequently to planning future matters.

We'll look at each of these elements in turn.

7.2 Scoping – the BOSCARDET framework

BOSCARDET is a mnemonic that can serve to scope any matter. It's a useful checklist both for taking instructions from the client and for internal planning purposes:

Table 1: The BOSCARDET framework

Background	What's the background to the project, and who are the key players?
Objectives	What's the purpose of the project?
Scope	What's included in the work?
Constraints	What limitations might affect project delivery?
Assumptions	What assumptions are the scoping and planning of the project based on?
Risks	What might make those assumptions incorrect?
Deliverables	What needs to be done, and by whom?
Estimate	What's the estimated cost?
Timing	What's the estimated timing?

7.3 Scheduling and resourcing

Scheduling and resourcing is an essential part of the planning and scoping stage. It involves dividing the job up as follows:

Table 2: Scheduling and resourcing

Phasing	Breaking the project down into phases and milestones
Workstreams	Identifying workstreams for each phase
Tasks	Identifying tasks within each phase and workstream
Team	Identifying the team members
Hours estimate	Estimating hours for each team member

A sample tasks and responsibilities list and sample resourcing and scheduling Gantt chart can be found in Appendix 3.

7.4 Costing and pricing

Fee negotiations are client-led games in which clients impose their will. That is the assumption which most lawyers make when formulating fee proposals. There is some truth in that assumption, of course, although it leads to the wrong approach, one which takes it as given that the law firm is at a disadvantage and can only win

"Most associates, and many partners, in commercial law firms have little or no idea of the margins they need to aim for, believing that winning work is more important than profitability if it will keep their teams busy. But what is good for utilisation may not be so good for time cost recovery rates or profit per lawyer (and consequently for profit per partner)."

work by underbidding. From experience, I know that a partner's first thoughts when bidding for work will be something like, "There are hungry competitors snapping at our heels who do this for a lot less than us; let's go for a discount and renegotiate later. We need the work to keep our hours and utilisation up." The mistake is not to ask instead the question, "What's this piece of work going to cost the firm, and what's our desired profit? Can we afford to do it at the market price?". Most associates, and many partners, in commercial law firms have little or no idea of the margins they need to aim for, believing that winning work is more important than profitability if it will keep their teams busy. But what is good for utilisation may not be so good for time cost recovery rates or profit per lawyer (and consequently for profit per partner).

Apart from the pitfalls of loss leading, there are the dangers of creeping discounts, that is, discounts on already-discounted time cost rates offered to panel clients where, once again, the temptation to bring in the deal trumps any rational fee analysis.

Most firms have simple costing and pricing tools that can and should be used to analyse the cost of a project and its profitability before a bid or quote is made. For more complex pieces of work, that analysis will be done by phase and workstream, using the information provided by the scheduling and resourcing exercise described in the previous section. A sample costing and pricing spreadsheet can be found in Appendix 3.

Once the analysis has been done, a range of negotiating strategies can be considered, including alternative fee arrangements (see section 6 of this chapter, "Business Awareness"), in the knowledge of how those arrangements will impact margins.

7.5 Monitoring, reporting and adapting

How to keep the right information flowing at the right time between firm and client and within the project team is an important part of planning. A crucial component is to ask the client how they wish to be kept informed: who needs to know what, how frequently does communication need to occur, and by what means? Diarising calls and meetings may appear bureaucratic, but these can always be cancelled if they don't need to take place. It's better to plan, agree and diarise communication than allow the natural instinct of busy lawyers – not to communicate well at all – to take over.

This is particularly important when it comes to cost reporting. Agreeing the content and frequency of cost reports in advance with the client, and maintaining the quality of cost information through the disciplined recording of time and disbursements and accurate narratives, is the surest way to manage client expectations and avoid unnecessary write-offs and unpaid fees. This is particularly true where – as is increasingly the case – procurement departments and fee audit specialists are involved, and real time cost and narratives are required by clients. In every matter team there should always be a person whose role it is – and who has the authority – to deal with the various aspects of cost reporting.

Internal information flow is often neglected. More often than not, there is poor communication between the group running a matter and other departments and offices about client instructions, transaction developments and strategy. This creates a sense that those other parties are mere subcontractors, and it can lead to lack of engagement, and frequently to cost overruns. This is because a lack of ownership of the client relationship is demotivating and discourages efficiency and cost discipline. I have found that the best way to deal with this is to nominate a person at the heart of the project team to act as the information hub, sending out and receiving updates and questions on a regular basis. This method works well alongside regular information meetings and conference calls.

7.6 Scope creep

Preventing scope creep – where the scope of the work changes and expands over the life of a project, and unexpected events that were not contemplated in the original project require to be dealt with – requires proper planning and communication. As long as it is agreed from the outset who is authorised to give scope change instructions, and both how and by whom the cost of those changes are to be agreed, then write-offs resulting from cost overruns will be minimised. Good communication, and bringing potential scope changes proactively to the attention of the client, are also key.

7.7 Review

Any piece of work is an opportunity to ask for, and give, feedback. As discussed in chapter III, section 4, "Communication, feedback and critical conversations", feedback catalyses trust if it takes the form of an honest, challenging conversation and if the parties are seen to apply the lessons learned to subsequent work. The process gives both clients and lawyers the opportunity to express their appreciation and opinions about what went well and what didn't go so well, and to feel valued by being heard. It is often botched for several reasons, including people simply not bothering to organise the review, or shying away from it through fear of criticism. When reviews do take place, lawyers usually see them as occasions for clients to tell them what they think (one-way feedback), whereas a key feature of a successful feedback conversation is that both sides should be given the opportunity to speak and be heard (reciprocal feedback). Sometimes the parties fail to ask questions but simply tell, or the review is treated as a box-ticking exercise with no effort being made to note and agree what each party will do better next time. These are all pitfalls to avoid.

Good feedback is not merely a one-off post-closing exercise with the client. At its best, feedback is actively and constantly solicited at all stages of a transaction so that it becomes a habit: little and often builds the best relationships.

8. Working effectively across borders

The following paragraphs are aimed primarily at London-based lawyers working with colleagues in other firms or offices. Their importance lies in the fact that international law firms often try to sell themselves on the basis of a single quality standard and joined-up approach across the globe. The fact is that lawyers don't do this well, and this is largely due to a failure to understand differences between jurisdictions, especially the different ways that people perceive and understand things.

8.1 Different perceptions

Ways of thinking, ways of doing

A couple of obvious points:

- People do not just speak a different language in other countries; they see and approach problems differently. For example, lawyers in some jurisdictions have a primarily rules-based approach and tend to reason deductively, from rule to conclusion. This contrasts with lawyers from common law jurisdictions, including the UK, whose approach tends to be more empirical and inductive, building solutions from precedent and general principles.
- Business – including legal business – is conducted differently in each jurisdiction. This is influenced by a wide range of factors, from the way institutions such as courts and governments function, to more subtle issues such as the importance of personal relations and the culture of autonomy versus collaborative working.

Deep-seated differences in thinking and in business culture can and do create communication problems and misunderstandings. When you add to the mix disparities in laws, legal systems and the ways people express themselves, the barriers to fluent communication and clear understanding look daunting. But they shouldn't be. The key to surmounting such obstacles is to create trust and understanding. Put yourself in the local counsels' shoes

"An instructing mail containing the phrase, 'If you are not an expert in [obscure area of law] please pass this on to your relevant specialist team' will not go down well if the local firm has never come across that area before. The message betrays a mother ship mentality and a lack of effort to see the world from the perspective of others."

and treat them as equal partners. And as in all successful working relationships, some of the essential ingredients include:

- establishing personal relations and maintaining them through regular contact;
- showing a willingness to understand differences; and
- a good dose of peripheral vision and inclusive behaviour.

8.2 Connecting across borders

On a day-to-day basis, building connections across borders means creating a dialogue; in other words, calling or meeting (not simply emailing) your local colleagues throughout a transaction. A partner should make the initial call to ensure that a relationship is established from the top and to make the local lawyer feel that he or she is being treated as an equal. That is essential to building trust and a good working relationship. What does not work is an impersonally drafted circular email from a trainee, sent out of the blue on a Friday evening, demanding a detailed response to a complicated multi-jurisdiction questionnaire by the following Monday.

On a longer term basis, the best way of building personal connections is through secondments, at both partner and associate level. Secondments will not always work out, as there is a risk that the secondee will remain both professionally and culturally isolated, but when they do they are a powerful way of forging a collegial network of personal connections that build trust and understanding. Regular participation in training programmes as well as specialist team and sector group meetings are also essential to sharing common values, methodology and ways of analysing problems.

8.3 Walking across borders in another's shoes

English law is not local law, and London market practice is not universal market practice. These are obvious points, but as anyone who has instructed lawyers abroad will recognise, there is often a tendency to assume that everyone does things in the way that you do them in your own jurisdiction, and that if they do not, they should. This attitude will not only generate misunderstandings – it will alienate the people you're working with.

It is also unhelpful to assume that your local colleague's firm will be organised in the same way as yours. It is a natural mistake to think, especially when working in the larger London firms, that their deep resources and waterfront expertise organised into specialist teams and sector groups will be reflected, somehow, in network offices and best friend firms. Of course, this isn't the case. An instructing mail containing the phrase, "If you are not an expert in [obscure area of law] please pass this on to your relevant specialist team" will not go

"An English turn of phrase might be misinterpreted, the latest Wall Street acronym or jargon may cause head-scratching, and the chances are that a quickfire, badly articulated monologue on a crackly conference call line will not be understood by local counsel at all."

down well if the local firm has never come across that area before. The message betrays a mother ship mentality and a lack of effort to see the world from the perspective of others.

8.4 Careful how you say it

The way in which communications, and particularly initial instructions, are tailored will convey the sender's sensitivity, or lack of it, to the differences mentioned above. Suggesting is productive (for example, "We are doing this in our jurisdiction; would that work in yours?"); dictating and imposing is not.

As a practical illustration, some jurisdictions don't have floating charges or a universal security register, and so there is little point in instructing colleagues in one of those jurisdictions to take security over all of a company's local assets under a standard English law debenture. If you do, you are more likely to get the simple, unhelpful response that it cannot be done, rather than a more constructive, solution-oriented reply prompted by open questions about what is possible under their legal system.

It is also worth noting that using clear, jargon-free and direct language in meetings, calls and emails will help considerably in creating proper communication and understanding, particularly where there is a language barrier. An English turn of phrase might be misinterpreted, the latest Wall Street acronym or jargon may cause head-scratching, and the chances are that a quickfire, badly articulated monologue on a crackly conference call line will not be understood by local counsel at all.

8.5 Inclusiveness and teamwork

Involve local lawyers throughout the transaction, where possible, as decision makers at the planning stage and in regular update meetings or conference calls thereafter. At a minimum, give clear instructions and obtain a transparent quote. Put them in front of the clients where practicable, and include them in team-wide email groups (there is often a tendency to confine these to the home office team). It is important to give them plenty of warning about changes to instructions and deadlines; it often helps to have a partner or senior associate tasked with the responsibility of actually calling to communicate important news peer-to-peer. Regular feedback and thanks when it is due are also important.

If all this is done successfully it will create buy-in and enthusiasm, and a joined-up team with considerable client service benefits. If it not done, local colleagues will feel that they are being treated as mere cogs in the machine, and it is more likely that they will fail to deliver on time and on budget through lack of engagement and ownership of the project or client relationship.

8.6 Appearing joined-up

A difficulty that often arises when dealing with local counsel is interpreting and passing on their advice in a form and style that the clients will want and that matches your firm's house style. This is challenging where the local advice is delivered in a lengthy memo in imperfect English and is lacking a practical, commercial edge. Often the most pragmatic solution is to prepare an executive summary of the advice for the client's consumption. But this will work only if the summary is submitted to the local counsel first. It is an unpleasant surprise (and this happens fairly often) for local counsel to discover that their advice has been paraphrased inaccurately and without their approval.

Another issue that arises in multi-jurisdictional, document-intensive transactions is duplication of contractual provisions, for example covenants and warranties, in the contracts for each jurisdiction. This results in unnecessary negotiations and imperfect matches from one jurisdiction to the next (particularly when local contracts are not in English). It therefore pays to plan the documentation carefully at an early stage with local counsel. An obvious and common solution is to keep the relevant provisions in a single master agreement, and strip them out of the local agreements.

IV. Self-leadership: getting the career you want

This chapter is about taking control of your career – thinking about what you want, as opposed to what's expected of you, and setting goals and steps for getting there. Much of the groundwork for this, particularly the self-assessment part, will be discussed in the early parts of the next chapter, about coaching yourself, and the succeeding chapter, about coaching others. Here we shall focus more on the nitty-gritty of building a career plan, and then making it happen.

1. Career possibilities – inside, outside, rock star

Partnership used to be the main – arguably the only – career goal available in a commercial law firm. Today partnership has become increasingly competitive, the path for getting there longer and more arduous, and the life of an equity partner shorter in the sense that participation in equity comes later in a partner's career and lasts for a shorter period, because of the equity book-ending phenomenon discussed in chapter II, section 2, "Money and lateral hires".

The good news is that the evolution of law firms, in particular the growth of non-legal professions within law firms, has created a number of alternative career possibilities for lawyers. Within the law firm itself, apart from traditional of counsel and legal director positions, these include roles in legal service centres, project management, knowledge management, learning and development and business development, as well as operational and management roles, both at the front line and at the C-suite level.

The size and shape of law firms will continue to change. Some of the top firms, those for whom achieving the highest level of profitability is the key driver, may cease to employ and train juniors and trainees because their large clients no longer want to pay for them. This will drive a trend away from the traditional pyramidal, highly geared, firm with lots of juniors at the bottom supporting a middle layer of experienced lawyers, with a few equity partners at the top. Firms will acquire a more cylindrical shape with less gearing, with fewer or no juniors and more closely matched numbers of experienced lawyers and equity partners. This may lead to the death of the 'up or out' model, and open up new roles for permanent senior lawyer positions. It may also reshape the remuneration structure in law firms.

Outside law firms there are in-house roles and flexible lawyer-on-demand roles, in addition to which an increasing number of lawyers appear to be moving into non-legal careers (what some refer to as the 'rock star' alternative – the term here being used in the loose sense of following your heart to do something completely different).[9] A lawyer or an alumnus in any of these positions will be valuable to a law firm

"It is therefore legitimate for lawyers to expect law firms to invest in their careers whether they want to become partners or not, and it makes sound sense for law firms to do so."

either by virtue of what they do within the firm (for those with an in-house role) or their ability to refer business and speak for the reputation of their *alma mater* (for those who move elsewhere). It is therefore legitimate for lawyers to expect law firms to invest in their careers whether they want to become partners or not, and it makes sound sense for law firms to do so.

2. Why make a plan?

Thinking about and writing down goals and actions increases self-awareness and a sense of control, which boosts focus and motivation. It's also helpful to see the writing of a career plan as a means to give shape and direction to your ambition and wishes, as opposed to a box-ticking exercise for the firm.

The planning process is a catalyst for reaching out, communicating and cooperating, creating synergies, building a support network and political capital. Testing personal vision and goals with colleagues will help you to clarify them and help others to buy into them.

The plan is a manifesto for your ambitions. Once written, it can serve as a way of holding yourself, and others, to account for the support pledged to help you implement your goals.

3. What should a good plan look like?

The plan is by definition personal and does not need to follow a rigid template. It's not about what others expect of you but rather where you want to take your practice and work–life balance. Starting is often the most difficult bit, so I've included a possible form of plan with some self-assessment questions in Appendix 2, which follows the three essential steps to producing an effective plan.

- Understand where you are now.
- Decide where you want to go and what the end point will look like.
- Define the actions that you will take, and the support that others will need to give you, in order to reach that point.

3.1 Where am I now?

The first step is self-assessment: where are you now? This is not a purely 'blank sheet' exercise: conversations inviting feedback and ideas from colleagues and even friends and family may produce helpful insights. Honest analysis of all aspects of your life will help you clarify your professional aspirations, even though you may decide not to include some of the more personal thinking in your final plan. Chapter V, sections 1–4, provide more detailed practical guidance on self-assessment.

It is sometimes very helpful in deciding where you are now, and where you should be going next, to write down your value proposition. A value proposition can take many forms, but its defining quality is that it should be brief, and convey a very clear and simple message about who you are, what you do and how that helps others or makes you outstanding. For example, Apple's value proposition for the iPhone is as follows:

Every iPhone we made – and we mean every single one – was built on the same belief. That a phone should be more than a collection of features. That above all, a phone should be absolutely simple, beautiful and magical to use.

The value proposition here – what makes an iPhone outstanding – is the user experience. What's yours?

An alternative is to write a small piece on who you are in 100 to 200 words. If you go through the exercise suggested in chapter V, section 2, "Self-assessment", and answer the questions in the first part of the career plan in Appendix 2, you will have some good material on which to draw: a description of your strengths, some adjectives which you and third parties use to describe you, and an understanding of what drives you and what gives you energy, recalling your proudest moments or when you were at your best. The idea is then to say in those 100 to 200 words:

- what you do;
- how you see yourself and how others see you;
- what your strengths, values and drivers are; and
- how those characteristics bring (or will bring) value to the work you do (or aspire to do).

For example, if listening and being supportive and empathetic are among your qualities, that could make you a good leader as well as a good client developer.

3.2 Where next?

The next step is fixing your objectives, both medium term (12 to 18 months) and long term (three to five years and beyond). This is about developing a positive, proactive, growth mindset: planting flags, visualising the path ahead and discovering the motivation that comes with that process. Sections 10 ("Knowing goals and managing expectations") and 11 ("Weighing up change") of chapter V provide practical guidance for formulating and visualising goals, but some key factors are set out below.

Effective goal-setting – key factors

- Know what you want. This should flow naturally from self-assessment and a good understanding of where you are now. You only have so much energy, so much time and so many resources: goal-setting is therefore also about doing less or letting go of some things in order to redirect your energy, time and resources elsewhere. A key question to consider is whether what you are doing inspires you and feels authentic.
- Understand the strategy, values and business objectives – of the firm, your group, industry sectors and region/office – and how your ambitions and goals align with them. This will be based on your reading of firm-wide, group, sector, and regional/office plans as well as discussions with other partners about their own plans.
- Understand the quality of your network and profile both within and outside the firm.
- Define a manageable number of realistic, time-based goals with clear success benchmarks. Bear in mind the SMART rule: goals should be Specific, Measurable, Achievable, Realistic and Time-based. A helpful question to ask in relation to any goal is, How will I know I've succeeded? Some examples are included in the career plan in Appendix 2.
- Identify the support you need to get there. This requires thinking about your support network and having full and open conversations to discuss your respective business plans. Understanding the mutual help that you can bring each other is key to creating buy-in and, in turn, making your goals a reality. There is a more detailed discussion of building internal and external and client networks in chapter III, section 5, "Building your connections".

3.3 Making it happen: commitments and follow-up

The last step is to commit to specific actions to achieve your goals. These should consist of immediate next steps and some specific, measurable actions to turn your ambitions into success.

Once you've written your plan, keep it alive. Revisit it to hold yourself and others to account. Have you done what you said you'd do? Have others given you the support they pledged? Tweak it – plans and objectives change.

It is also important to set regular dates for discussing progress with your supporters and key stakeholders in your future. This will foster a sense of involvement and ownership on their part and reinforce a sense of partnership and shared goals which will have been created in discussions at the time of the plan's conception. Regular discussions will also ensure that you, and the members of your support network, are held to account.

"From a partner's or a practice group's perspective, the ability to put forward successful partnership candidates is akin to reproductive selection in the Darwinian sense: those who are able to do so ensure their legacy, and in a law firm only those with political power and financial vigour will pass on their genes."

4. What does it take to make partner?

4.1 Politics and Darwinism

The process of achieving partnership in law firms is fraught with tension and mystery. Although most law firms have a process which is more or less transparent, who gets put forward, selected for the running and ultimately elected is normally the result of subjective judgement by those who count: partners with political clout and profitable practices.

From a partner's or a practice group's perspective, the ability to put forward successful partnership candidates is akin to reproductive selection in the Darwinian sense: those who are able to do so ensure their legacy, and in a law firm only those with political power and financial vigour will pass on their genes. Because partnership, and in particular equity, is a limited resource, competition among the partners to push their candidates is sometimes fierce.

What does that mean for candidates? It means that they should, above all, ensure they have the right sponsors among the partners – people who will act both as champions (in that they will be personally invested in the cause and risk political capital) and as articulate advocates for their candidacy. This also militates strongly for the importance of building a network, a point discussed in greater detail in chapter III, section 5, "Building your connections".

4.2 Personal attributes

There are so many different types of partners in law firms, some excellent, some deeply flawed, that the optimist can rightly point out that anybody can make it. Drawing on my many years' experience with law firm partners, I can say that the ideal partnership candidate has a number of essential characteristics, as below.

Attributes of strong partnership candidates

A good candidate will:

- possess strong emotional intelligence and a growth mindset;
- demonstrate natural leadership qualities, including a willingness to:
  1. listen, communicate well and solicit views;
  2. make the effort to have regular feedback meetings with their team and stay in regular touch with their clients;
  3. talk to and not about their colleagues, be consistently supportive and non-judgemental, and embrace diversity; and
  4. set an example through integrity and high professional and ethical standards.
- be personally invested in mentoring and training;
- have energy and ambition;
- be highly commercial and understand clients' businesses and needs;
- be a sector expert and a recognised go-to person in their area of expertise;
- be a solid project manager and good at delegation and getting things done competently;
- be credible and reliable, build trust quickly and have strong relationships at senior levels in their client organisations;
- have strong business development skills and a self-sustaining practice;
- understand the firm and their group well, have a good grasp of values and strategy, and be well known and liked within and outside the firm;
- have judgement and intellect (more of the former than the latter), clarity of thinking and the ability to break problems down into manageable components;
- have competent (but not necessarily more than that) legal skills;
- have a clear understanding of what their work–life balance should be;
- have clear personal and professional goals and a vision for where they want to take their practice as a partner; and
- have curiosity and a breadth of interests, personability, and humour – for me, these last attributes are non-negotiable.

4.3 Economics

Budgeting, billing and worrying about financial KPIs are rarely the province of the associate. As a result, partnership candidates often struggle with putting together cogent financial forecasts for their practice in their candidacy papers. However, most hard-working senior associates will see a large part of their practice drying up when they become partners and start competing with those who previously fed them work. Partnership candidates must therefore demonstrate that they have a strong business case and a self-sustaining practice, backed by a consistent track record of billings, utilisation and profitability.

4.4 Vision

A partnership candidate needs to demonstrate that he or she thinks like a partner, and can formulate a coherent vision of the size and shape, profitability and focus of their practice and their team over a short- and medium-term horizon. "I'll continue doing what I've done well in the past and see where it takes me" won't cut it. A vision demonstrating clear goals and ambitions is essential. The vision for practice growth should be backed by cogent economic forecasts. Above all, that vision and those forecasts must demonstrate a profitability at least consistent with the firm's targets – see chapter III, section 6.3, "Profitability: what associates need to know".

4.5 Luck

However strong a candidacy may be on paper, it will often founder on the shoals of economic adversity such as a downturn in the candidate's sector of expertise, a dip in the firm's fortunes or a recession. I have always advised associates to plan their careers so that they have a 'major', an area of expertise which is the key part of their practice and in which they have recognition both within the firm and in the market, and a 'minor' which will give them more exposure within the firm and enable them to bolster their financial track record if necessary, or develop into their major in the case of an economic downturn. For example, a candidate might develop a major in white collar crime, and a minor in general commercial litigation.

Conversely, a candidate who might not be ideal on paper may be lucky enough to have a profitable practice, or the necessary expertise at the right place and time to make them an irresistible candidate. In an ideal world, associates should look ahead and seek out areas that will develop into profitable niche practices, and orient their careers accordingly. After all, you can make you own luck or, as Louis Pasteur put it more elegantly, luck smiles only on the well-prepared.

V. Coaching yourself and others through change

Having looked at some of the factors that shape legal careers, leadership in law firms and self-authoring one's career, in the next two chapters we'll look at coaching oneself and others through that career. We'll examine self-awareness and self-management issues like emotional intelligence, agile thinking and motivation, as well as the changes that a lawyer is likely to face in a professional lifetime.

The coaching plan illustrated in Figure 2 starts from the middle, with self-discovery, before moving out in concentric circles to an understanding of others and their perceptions, and then to an appreciation of the wider context and environment. Finally, it shifts into the future with the formulation of goals and plans for a successful career. Among the core ideas in this chapter, echoing themes discussed above, are that successful individuals know and are comfortable with who they are; that they seek constant feedback; and that they set themselves goals.

1. Visiting the oracle

In ancient Greece, those visiting Delphi in the hope of obtaining oracular guidance would be met by the exhortation, "γνῶθι σεαυτόν" – "Know thyself" – inscribed above the entrance to the Temple of Apollo. Like the pronouncements of the oracle, this meant different things to different people. One interpretation might be that it pays to

Figure 2: The coaching plan

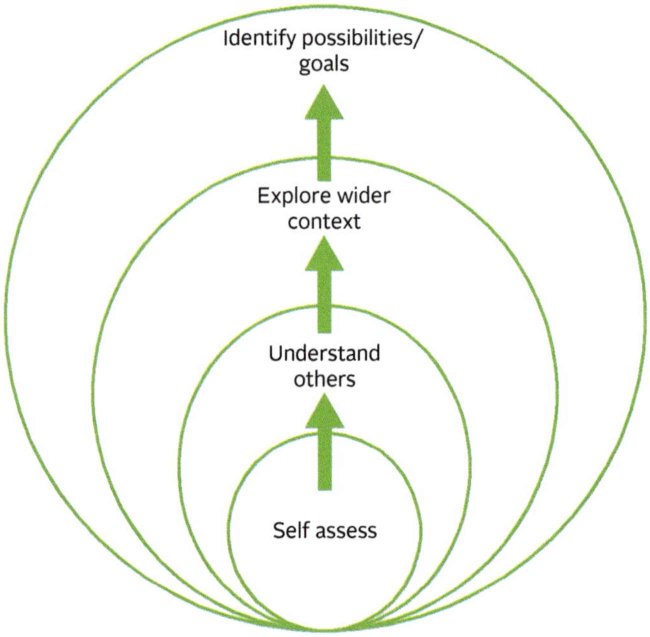

know yourself before looking for answers elsewhere, as many of those answers will come spontaneously through self-awareness. One of coaching's primary aims is to raise self-awareness, as this creates choice, which in turn builds confidence and autonomy. These are the essential steps in embarking on any journey. Self-awareness-raising tools will help build a picture of how the coached see themselves, how they deal and engage with others and how others see and engage with them.

2. Self-assessment

Before starting a coaching assignment I will often ask a coachee to do some self-reflection homework. It might sometimes be helpful to start with a strengths survey. I have used Strengths Profile,[10] CliftonStrengths assessment,[11] and Via.[12] I also ask clients to do the following:

- invite colleagues, friends and family to describe you in a few words or to give you an example of when they saw you at your best;
- write about your three proudest moments; and
- prepare a personal statement or sales pitch describing your key strengths (for the new role, for example) in 100 to 200 words.

This preparation will enable the coachee to hit the ground running from the first coaching session. It is a particularly useful way to prepare for coaching around confidence, resilience and profile-building. These issues will often come up in transition coaching.

3. Anchors and drivers

A useful aspect of any self-assessment exercise in a change context is to build an understanding of anchors and drivers. There are several tools available. Schein's Career Anchors is useful for identifying the one thing (among eight anchors) that you would not give up if you had to make a series of tough choices about your career.[13]

I also find David Rock's SCARF model helpful.[14] This was developed out of neuroscience studies on social needs. SCARF stands for Status, Certainty, Autonomy, Relatedness and Fairness.

These models can help raise a coachee's awareness about what really matters to them in a work context. It will help them to gain a perspective on the energising and energy-draining factors in their current environment, and the factors that will matter in any post-transition environment.

4. Values and simple guiding principles

Among the key goals of any self-assessment exercise (and which the homework and tools mentioned above should help uncover) is to understand core values and simple guiding principles. For example, what are the values that you live by? Or to put it another way, what situations make you uncomfortable in a professional context, and in your life outside work? Honesty, respect, and who matters most to you are examples of core values. What principles or views guide you? "You make your own luck" or "Persistence pays" are examples of simple guiding principles which, together with your core values and principles, act as a lodestone governing your behaviours and decisions. Ascertaining them is not about making moral judgements about yourself, but rather knowing, and accepting, who you are and what makes you tick.

5. Motivation

Optimism and hope are key predictors of success. Many people are natural optimists, and when you listen to them what you hear is a narrative, a way of explaining the world and themselves, through stories and constructs that generally predict success and fulfilment. Everyone relies on stories and constructs to interpret the past and present and to predict the future, and the narratives that people create to explain their failures and successes will colour their predictions with either optimism or resignation. Hope and optimism are intimately connected with motivation because they represent a mindset where the fear of failure plays very little part, where not succeeding is seen as a learning opportunity, where persistence pays and where possibilities are there to be explored and embraced.

For those of us who are not natural optimists, the good news is that optimism and motivation can be learned. According to the theory of self-efficacy as formulated by the psychologist Albert Bandura, optimism and motivation result from moving outside your comfort zone and achieving mastery of a particular skill.[15] This applies at many levels, from the physical to the intellectual, from learning and mastering a game to a subject, trade, sport or profession. The idea is that as we engage with a challenge, we may "fail" at first, possibly many times, but as we learn and gradually master the challenge we feel better about ourselves, develop a sense of enjoyment, a feeling that the activity is rewarding and the motivation to do more. This idea is connected with 'flow', or being in the zone. The concept of flow was named by Mihaly Csikszentmihalyi, and involves a state in which a person engages in a particular intellectual or physical task in almost trance-like total absorption.[16] Flow also involves mastery: in a state of flow there is a perfect balance between challenge, doing and mastery. Too little challenge means boredom, too much creates anxiety.[17] Mastering challenges and small wins trigger the reward centres in our brains, bringing a sense of wellbeing and satisfaction and making us want to repeat the process.

"It's worth noting that purpose is intimately connected with goal-setting which, along with the regular solicitation of feedback, is a hallmark of high achievers."

Daniel H Pink, in his 2011 book *Drive – The Surprising Truth About What Motivates Us*,[18] proposes that in situations where people are fairly paid, intrinsic motivation is based on mastery (the drive to become competent and the need for achievement), autonomy and purpose. While in my experience the first two conditions are often easily met in a legal career, lawyers often find it more difficult to create the third condition – purpose – because they are poor at visualising possibilities and formulating a vision of the future. When, through coaching or other support, they find the confidence and ability to do so, this turns out to be a powerful source of purpose and motivation. It's worth noting that purpose is intimately connected with goal-setting which, along with the regular solicitation of feedback, is a hallmark of high achievers.

So motivation is essential to coping with change, and to making change happen, for two main reasons:

- the motivation to make the transition is key to success; and
- the motivation to do the things necessary to bring about the change and to adopt and embed new behaviour is equally important.

Edward L Deci and Richard Ryan's theory of self-determination is interesting in this context. It proposes a link between motivation and the need for autonomy, competence and relatedness. It also examines the distinction between intrinsic and extrinsic motivators. One of Deci's findings is that giving people unexpected positive feedback on a task increases their intrinsic motivation to do it, because that feedback fulfils their need for competence.[19]

Motivating others – the essential leadership quality – means understanding and creating conditions where people can satisfy their need for mastery and achievement, a sense of belonging, a feeling of control, and the ability to live up to their ideals and values. We'll come back to this in the context of emotional intelligence, discussed in section 7 below.

6. Readiness for change

An important self-awareness issue to be considered in any transition is readiness for change. Prochaska's Stages of Change model may be useful here.[20] The model divides the change process into five stages. It is applicable to many types of change, including career transitions and habit or behavioural change. It is helpful for the coachee (and the coach) to understand that these stages exist and to identify the stage at which the coachee finds themselves. The coachee may then feel more comfortable if, for example, they feel any doubts about the change or do not yet consider themselves ready to move on. The stages are as follows:

"Motivating others – the essential leadership quality – means understanding and creating conditions where people can satisfy their need for mastery and achievement, a sense of belonging, a feeling of control, and the ability to live up to their ideals and values."

Prochaska's Stages of Change model

1 *Pre-contemplation:* The coachee may not have considered change. The coach can help raise awareness by asking questions around how things might improve, and the implications for the coachee of not changing.

2 *Contemplation:* The coachee may have seen the need for change, but remains ambivalent about it. The coach can help explore that ambivalence and possibly the reasons behind it.

3 *Preparation:* The coachee has made the decision to change but is still exploring whether he or she wants the change and is still thinking about the way forward.

4 *Action:* Steps are being taken to make the change. Here the coaching can support the planning and goal-setting process and monitor results.

5 *Relapse to a previous stage:* Should this occur, the coach can reassure the coachee that this is normal.

6 *Maintenance:* The action towards change or changed behaviour is maintained for a sustained period.

7 *Termination:* The change has taken place or the modified behaviour has permanently taken hold.

Readiness for change is of course linked to many things discussed in this Special Report, among them confidence, optimism and growth mindset. It is also influenced by the flexibility of thinking styles. On this subject I can do no better than encourage you to read Isaiah Berlin's *The Hedgehog and the Fox*[21] and Leonard Mlodinow's *Elastic*.[22] *The Hedgehog and the Fox* proposes that people are divided into two types of thinkers: hedgehogs, who tend to see the world through a single overarching idea, construct or paradigm, and foxes, who draw on a variety of sources for their world view. *Elastic* is an excellent discussion of thinking styles and the science behind them, and in particular of agile thinkers, who are comfortable with contradiction and ambiguity, and who Mlodinow calls 'hoppers'.

7. Emotional intelligence

When I look at strong leaders – people who carry others with them – what I notice is that they have three qualities: a strong faith or belief, an almost uncanny understanding of what people want, and an ability to echo that understanding back to their followers. These qualities can best be understood through a discussion of emotional intelligence.

Emotional intelligence is a concept which gained popularity from the 1990s thanks to Daniel Goleman, who has written a series of books on the subject.[23] His model rests on five pillars:

- self-awareness;
- self-management;
- motivation;
- empathy; and
- social awareness.

I would argue that emotional intelligence trumps intellectual ability, expertise and even experience as a predictor of success, although experience does inform and shape emotional intelligence. Even though all facets of emotional intelligence are essential qualities in a good leader, people who lack them often get promoted into leadership positions for other reasons, such as technical expertise or ambition.

Emotional intelligence is something that some people possess naturally, like optimism (which is in fact a facet of emotional intelligence). The good news for those who are not naturally emotionally intelligent is that it can be acquired to a great extent by learning and self-reflection, and by practising its precepts.

The sections that follow examine the five pillars in more detail.

7.1 Self-awareness

In earlier sections we have discussed self-awareness in the context of practical tools for assessing drivers, values and principles. I believe that real self-awareness leads to self-acceptance, and to being comfortable with yourself. This involves knowing your values and where you want to go; knowing your simple guiding principles; being able to express your emotions; self-compassion and letting go. All these things require receptivity, that is, the ability to notice your emotional state and be receptive to it. They require listening – to yourself and (as discussed both above and below) to others. Creating physical spaces, activities and intervals of time in your working day for noticing is a good start. We'll discuss this in more detail in chapter 7, "Wellbeing", below.

7.2 Self-management

Self-management is about recognising and managing internal states and disruptive emotions such as impulses. The key step towards managing these is to be conscious of them and accept them for what they are. Good self-management leads to trustworthiness, conscientiousness and adaptability.

"Attunement often happens unconsciously, but if we are aware of what is going on, it can become a powerful way of managing personal interactions and creating strong bonds of trust."

7.3 Motivation

We've discussed motivation above. Goleman identifies four factors under the heading of motivation:

- achievement drive;
- commitment to one's own or group goals;
- initiative and opportunism; and
- optimism in the face of challenges or setbacks.

7.4 Empathy

Empathy is about understanding and being attuned to the emotions and needs of others.

7.5 Social skills

This heading is about adeptness at inducing desirable responses in others and involves influencing, communication, conflict management, collaboration, change management, teamwork and leadership.

7.6 Reading people

Many of the aspects of emotional intelligence are discussed in greater depth in other parts of this Special Report, but it's worth devoting a few paragraphs here to emotional attunement or mirroring.

Attunement and mirroring are processes that occur where a person knows that emotions are met with empathy, accepted and reciprocated. They are at the heart of emotional connection and trust. Examples include the interaction between a parent and child, a successful politician and his followers, and a good listener and conversation partner.

The process of emotional attunement is natural because emotions are contagious. Attunement often happens unconsciously, but if we are aware of what is going on, it can become a powerful way of managing personal interactions and creating strong bonds of trust. Coordination of emotions is the essence of rapport. This involves actively noticing the other person's emotional state as well as one's own, and being receptive to both; in other words, taking them as they are without judgement or criticism. Emotional receptivity requires calmness, which in turn requires self-awareness and mastery of one's own emotions.

The related process of mirroring involves signalling to the other person that one is receptive to their emotional state by literally reflecting back their behaviour, such as their body language, tone of voice or turn of phrase.

Understanding and mastering attunement and mirroring is the foundation of four essential interpersonal leadership skills:

- organising groups;
- negotiating solutions;
- making personal connections; and
- analysing and understanding others' feelings and motives.

When managing a group, checking in with the mood of the group by hearing what the members have to say, and how they say it, before mirroring back and then setting out one's own position is an effective leadership technique. These techniques can, of course, be used to set the emotional tone of a conversation by actively bringing down the temperature of another person's emotional state or, in the case of politicians, raising the emotional temperature by (for example) using language that stokes people's innate fears, and a tone that catalyses anxiety.

8. Walking in another's shoes

Having coached the client around the question, "What do I know about myself?", the next stage in the coaching plan is to look at the question, "How do I interact with people and my work environment?" We will start with feedback and 360° reviews before looking at tools and techniques for exploring and demystifying interpersonal perceptions.

8.1 Feedback and 360° reviews

I find it helpful, before embarking on a coaching assignment, to conduct a bespoke feedback exercise by interviewing colleagues of the coachee at various seniority levels. These interviews can be conducted in person or by phone, will generally last about 20 to 30 minutes, and will deal with three questions.

- What is X doing well?
- What might X do more of?
- What might X do less of?

I contract with the interviewee on confidentiality by stating that what I am told will not be fed back on an attributed basis, but will form part of an anonymised report which I will prepare using my own words and drawing on the results of other interviews; and that the report will be delivered to the coachee and nobody else. I also undertake to the coachee and the firm that neither the report, nor the conversations on which it is based, will be disclosed to the firm or other third parties without the coachee's consent. The report can be debriefed alongside the latest annual appraisals, recent 360° survey and/or assessment centre results if available, and the outcome of a three-way session with a line manager if relevant. Together these will form an excellent support to inform self-awareness coaching around strengths and development areas as perceived by the coachee, and also by others. Identifying blind spots (ie, differences between the coachee's and third-party perceptions) is also an essential product of this exercise.

8.2 Taking it impersonally

A potential difficulty with feedback and discussions of others' perceptions is that both feedback and perceptions can be taken personally. It is extremely helpful in this context to conduct a psychometric assessment exercise with the coachee. This is particularly useful in illustrating and explaining how differences in individual behaviour, preferences and needs contribute to very different perceptions that we all have of each other and of the world. It depersonalises sensitive feedback messages and helps coachees to understand that "It's not me, it's the way others see things".

8.3 Perceptual Positions

Among the several possible "walking in another's shoes" exercises, the Perceptual Positions exercise is one that I find particularly helpful where there are difficult interpersonal issues or awkward team dynamics. The way it works is as follows: the coachee describes the issue, reactions and feelings from their perspective, then from the point of view of one or more other protagonists, and then from the point of view of a detached observer. This will lead to insights where none were available when stuck in a single frame of reference.

The exercise can do a lot to defang a difficult interpersonal problem and help the coachee, by exploring a different perspective, to prepare for a critical conversation or simply carry a lighter load.

8.4 Looking through the Johari Window

Among the many different tools to help with self-assessment and understanding how communication and feedback might be helpful, my favourite is the Johari Window, created by US psychologists Joseph Luft and Harrington Ingham.[24]

Figure 3: The Johari Window

	Known to self	Not known to self
Known to others	Arena	Blind spot
Not known to others	Façade	Unknown

The coachee picks a number of adjectives to describe themselves, and then asks half a dozen or so friends, family and/or colleagues to provide a similar number of adjectives to describe the coachee. Adjectives chosen by both the coachee and others will go into the Arena. Adjectives chosen only by the coachee go into the Façade, which contains information known only to the coachee and not others. Adjectives chosen only by others belong to the Blind Spot, which contains information about others' perceptions of the coachee which may not be shared with the coachee. The aim of good communication and feedback is to increase the size of the Arena.

9. Mapping the environment

9.1 Becoming an environmentalist

Transition coaching in any organisation is not properly done without the coachee acquiring a full understanding of context. The next stage in our coaching plan is therefore to help the coachee map their context. By 'context' I mean the day-to-day workplace environment and the interpersonal dynamics involving immediate colleagues (what I will call the local neighbourhood), but also broadening out to include the wider firm's culture, values, strategy and challenges, the political forces at play within the firm and the place of the firm in the market (what I will call the wider universe).

In a transition from one role to another or one office or firm to another, that same mapping exercise can be conducted not only for the current environment, but for the future environment as well, the aim being to be able to answer the following questions.

Mapping the context – questions for the coachee

- What aspects of my current local neighbourhood play to my strengths, values and fulfilment, and what aspects do not work for me?
- What does my support network look like today, and what will it be in the new role?
- What aspects of my future local neighbourhood will be positive or negative, energising or draining?
- How does the wider universe influence what I am doing today?
- How will the wider universe impact what I will be doing, my goals and what is expected of me in, say, one year and five years?
- How can I shape my new role in a way that works for me?
- How can I engage with my future environment (both at the local neighbourhood and wider universe level) to influence it in a way that will work for me?

9.2 Breaking it down

Many of the answers will be evident from the earlier stages of the coaching plan, including the self-assessment and feedback. Those that are not will require the coachee to do some thinking, and reach out to their network (or even beyond it) to ask questions. The point here is to help the coachee think about the new role not simply as an extension of the existing one, but one in which the context will be vitally important. It is a small step then to appreciate that investigating that context and engaging with it early are vital components of transition planning. This is essentially about taking a wide view, taking the initiative and control, and thinking politically.

9.3 Keeping it up

Once in the new role, continuing self-assessment, feedback and communication can be used to review the map of the new local neighbourhood and wider universe. That will then inform the

"Once the coachee has a good understanding of themselves and the environment – and their interaction with it – the next step is to fix goals and commit to them in writing. Nobody gets into a cab and says, 'Drive!', except in the movies."

adjustments that the coachee could make to their behaviour, habits and support network to adapt better to the new environment and ensure a successful integration. The temptation is often instead to replicate previous behaviours and habits in the new environment, and hope for the best. As we have already seen, this is particularly true when entire teams relocate to new firms. The danger there is the oil and water phenomenon – failure by the new team to reach out, communicate, adjust and mix will lead to tribalism and mistrust and, ultimately, an unsuccessful transplant.

10. Knowing goals and managing expectations

10.1 Where do you want to go?

Once the coachee has a good understanding of themselves and the environment – and their interaction with it – the next step is to fix goals and commit to them in writing. Nobody gets into a cab and says, "Drive!", except in the movies. This is not about committing rigidly to a plan. It is about developing the future mindset: planting flags, visualising the path ahead and discovering the self-motivation that comes with that process. Reality, as it plays out, will of course be different: life is what happens when you make plans.

10.2 Goal-oriented questions

Fixing goals comes in several flavours, ranging from writing a personal business plan with performance and business development targets for the following year to answering broader questions, for example:

- What would I like my work–life balance to look like in the next year and in three to five years (and perhaps beyond)?
- What do I want each of my four dimensions as a lawyer (Thinker, Doer, Developer, Supporter – see chapter VI, section 2.1) to look like?
- What difference would I like to make in my new role?

10.3 Great expectations

There is another line of useful questions around communication and managing expectations.

- What is expected of me, and do those expectations match my goals?
- What have I communicated to others about my goals and what I believe is expected of me?
- Have I tested my assumptions of what is expected of me?

These questions go hand in hand with the feedback, environmental mapping and goal-setting described in previous sections.

10.4 Visualisation

Goal-setting is not always an easy task, particularly for lawyers whose immediate task focus often relegates proper planning to a secondary role. Visualisation can be a helpful tool to get the ball rolling, the questions that I find helpful being as follows.

- What will it look like to be in the new role (eg, as a newly promoted partner)?
- Can you describe how a typical day might unfold, from start to finish?
- What will you feel in your new role?
- What will your work–life balance look like?
- What will your important personal relationships look like, both outside and in work?
- What will success look and feel like?

11. Weighing up change

There are many helpful questions, methods and tools for weighing up a move or change. Some of these are described briefly below.

11.1 Motivations

Where the move is voluntary, useful questions for the coachee might be:

- What are my real motivations for moving?
- Could I satisfy those motivations in my current role/firm, or only in the new role/firm?
- Could I change things to the way I want them here?

11.2 SWOT analysis

It might be helpful to convert a simple pros and cons list into a SWOT analysis – Strengths, Weaknesses, Opportunities and Threats. Strengths and weaknesses are things which are innate to the coachee or which are within the coachee's control. Opportunities and threats are things that may happen but that are outside the coachee's control. It may be easier to break the change down into headings or objectives, and do a SWOT per objective. For example, higher remuneration might be one objective, and professional development another. A SWOT grid is illustrated below. A similar grid, which includes useful self-assessment questions, in included in Appendix 1.

Figure 4: SWOT analysis

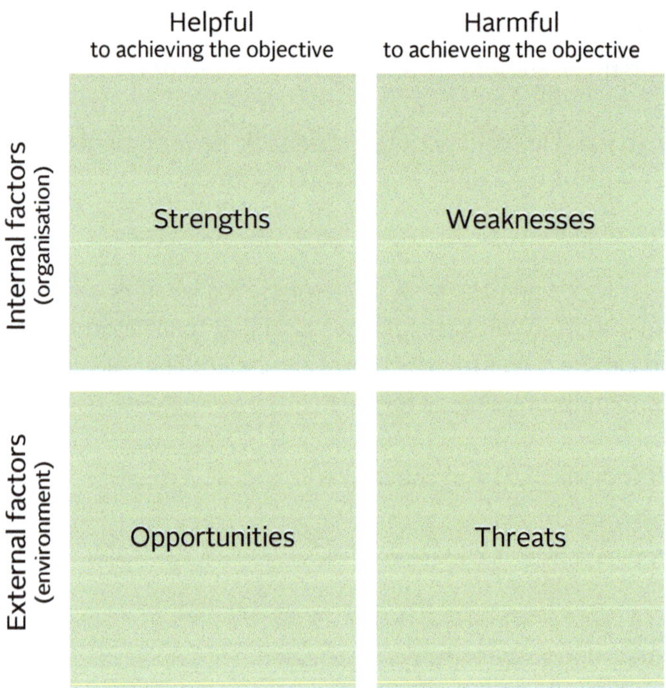

11.3 Optionality

In thinking things through before a move or change, the coachee might ask themselves:

- What options am I gaining/can I gain here (long term and short term)?
- What options am I closing off?

Take as an example a fixed share partner looking to move firms to take up an offer of equity. That equity offer from another firm might be leveraged in the short term in negotiations to obtain equity at the current firm, which will widen the coachee's options. The move can also, in the medium/long term, make it easier for the coachee to move to another equity partnership elsewhere at a later date. On the other hand, moving to the new firm may narrow the coachee's lifestyle options in the short and medium term because of the energy and time that will have to be diverted to building a new practice (albeit the move may broaden those options in the long term because extra remuneration may enable improvements in other areas).

11.4 Nurturing vs draining analysis

It may be useful to look at the move or change in terms of its energising or de-energising (or draining) effects. Questions here might be:

- What will be nurturing about the move (ie, what will energise me and play to my strengths, enjoyment or fulfilment)?
- Conversely, what will be draining or de-energising?

11.5 Balance sheet

This is a variant on a standard list of pros and cons. The coachee simply writes what he or she stands to gain (both tangible gains, such

"Coaching will naturally lead to an understanding of choices, and the autonomy that comes from the ability to exercise those choices. That in itself is a great source of self-confidence."

as remuneration, and intangible gains, such as happiness or fulfilment) on the assets side of the balance sheet, and what he or she stands to lose on the liabilities side. On the liabilities side the coachee should also include the extra time and energy required to make the move a success. Then (and this is the real difference from the standard pros and cons list) the coachee should ascribe a points value to each item.

11.6 Project management analysis

This brings together some of the other analyses. The coachee might consider the following questions.

- What are my objectives in making the move?
- What is the scope of my new role going to be?
- What are the assumptions I am making about the move, and are they realistic?
- What are the risks I am taking in making this move?
- What are the concrete things I need to do to make this a success?
- How do I define success?
- What is the time frame for success?
- Can I realistically achieve success in the time frame?

12. Confidence

Coaching for change often involves coaching for confidence. The change itself may be a source of concern based on limiting beliefs, which in turn may hold the coachee back from doing the things which may be necessary to navigate transition successfully. Coaching will naturally lead to an understanding of choices, and the autonomy that comes from the ability to exercise those choices. That in itself is a great source of self-confidence.

12.1 Confidence and the art of networking and profile-building

A perennial confidence-related issue in transition coaching is networking and profile-building. The ability to do both is a precondition to successful change partly for political reasons (building a strong, wide support network) and partly for business development purposes. This ability rests partly on the confidence to reach out, make and nurture contacts, and advertise successes. What holds coachees back most here is the perception that they are having to convince others that they are worthy of attention. This, with the attendant fear of rejection, is a powerful demotivator. Good coaching can replace this perception with the understanding that successful networking depends not so much on selling oneself as showing others that you are interested in them. For that reason, the art of networking is largely asking others questions about themselves, which can be as simple as, "What's on your mind right now?" That makes the initial approach much easier, as all you need is to find the excuse to have the

"Humility is not a good publicist. People don't bother to inquire or find out about others' achievements unless they have to, although good leaders should do so."

conversation. Coaching will also help coachees understand their own drivers and others' perceptions of their qualities, which will help them become comfortable with delivering a narrative about themselves that comes across as genuine and engaging.

12.2 Ringing the bell

The issue of advertising success is one I come across more often when coaching lawyers than non-lawyers. Although it appears counter-intuitive, lawyers are often averse to publicising and celebrating their own successes internally while finding it much easier – in some cases innately so – to do the same thing with clients. Yet it is an essential component of internal profile-building, and team-building as well.

There exists a tendency to believe that people within an organisation will get to hear of one's successes and contributions, as if the hard work and skill that one puts into them endows them with magical self-publicising virtues. Somehow, these successes will inevitably get them noticed by colleagues and partners. They won't. Humility is not a good publicist. People don't bother to inquire or find out about others' achievements unless they have to, although good leaders should do so. And don't rely on others doing it for you: you are responsible for building your own profile just as much as taking control of your own career. Only actively bringing achievements to people's attention will work, so the key to profile-raising is to make a habit of dropping one's achievements and successes into conversations and sending out messages to ring the bell. For those who worry about coming across as narcissists, one of the best ways of ringing the bell is to celebrate the achievement of the team – it doesn't need to be done by a partner, but by any team member – by communicating successes to other departments, sector group teams and clients. Another way of advertising a successful transaction, case or piece of work is to promote it as a knowledge-sharing opportunity. However you do it, tell a story, make it engaging, and make it about others as well as yourself.

12.3 Self-compassion

We are our own worst critics. I unashamedly advocate mindfulness here. Practising mindfulness will bring acceptance, and self-acceptance in particular. Self-compassion, accepting yourself as you are and self-forgiveness can be very powerful in removing barriers to achievement and building confidence and positive self-worth.

12.4 Impostor syndrome

It is often said that we see ourselves as better than we are. There is another category of people – quite a large one to judge from many self-confessed high-achieving celebrities, and a particularly large one

"If you believe that effort, learning and experience are ends in themselves rather than merely means to success, then fear of failure is no longer a problem. Indeed, 'failure' becomes, for the growth mindsetter, an enriching experience and an opportunity to learn what to adjust and improve."

in law firms judging from my own experience – who are afflicted by impostor syndrome. The term was first used (as 'impostor phenomenon') in a 1978 article, "The impostor phenomenon in high-achieving women: Dynamics and therapeutic intervention", by Pauline R Clarence and Suzanne A Imes.[25] At the heart of impostor syndrome lies a perceived lack of personal ability which makes it difficult to accept that personal success is due to one's competence, skill and ability. Because of this perception, success gives rise to fears that one will be exposed as a fraud, undeserving of the success. Much can be done, through counselling and even coaching, to alleviate impostor syndrome, including learning self-acceptance and a willingness to receive and believe compliments and positive feedback.

12.5 Growth mindset and resilience

No examination of the topic of confidence would be complete without at least a brief discussion of 'growth mindset', a concept made famous by Carol Dweck.[26] She contrasts two groups:

- people with a fixed mindset, who tend to believe that attributes leading to success, such as talent and intelligence, are fixed and innate; and
- people with a growth mindset, who believe that intelligence and talent can grow through learning and experience.

Dweck encourages parents and teachers to praise effort rather than success. This shifts the emphasis away from results as the only mark of success in a child's or student's mind, and towards the process of learning. If you believe that effort, learning and experience are ends in themselves rather than merely means to success, then fear of failure is no longer a problem. Indeed, "failure" becomes, for the growth mindsetter, an enriching experience and an opportunity to learn what to adjust and improve. A fixed mindsetter will tend to dwell on the failure itself and see it as an indictment of his or her abilities, eroding confidence, or as an injustice, fostering resentment. A growth mindset is therefore a key ingredient in resilience, because growth mindsetters will not only survive "failures" but thrive on the learning they bring.

The idea of growth mindset also connects strongly with motivation, discussed in section 5 of this chapter, and particularly with the notion of the virtuous circle of challenge, mastery and flow. It also connects with the way that successful athletes prepare, their emphasis being on process and discipline as the means to improvement rather than an exclusive focus on winning.

VI. Change in a lawyer's career

1. Types of change and their challenges

1.1 The future mindset

As surely as death and taxes, a lawyer will face several seniority transitions in the course of his or her career. A key ingredient in these transitions is forging a future mindset, that is, understanding and thinking oneself into the new role. Many lawyers assume that seniority transitions are just an extension of their existing roles. The gradual, linear nature of many transitions feeds that illusion. So when asked how they see themselves a few years into the new role, most lawyers will describe the future in terms of what they do already. The role of a good coach is to help the coachee really understand, visualise and 'live' the new role so that he or she can mentally plan and grow into it proactively over a period of time.

1.2 Changing practice areas and retooling

As the markets evolve and law firms seek to meet strategic goals, every lawyer will almost inevitably be called upon to specialise in a different practice area or change their practice mix at least once, if not several times, in their career. The challenges here include acquiring new skills, a new track record and new clients. This can amount to a radical reinvention of one's professional identity. Many of the coaching issues here involve confidence, building internal and external support and profile-raising. They also involve learning how to leverage existing skills, support and client networks to grow into the new practice area; developing a growth mindset; and understanding how learning and experimentation can be a source of enthusiasm and motivation.

1.3 Moving offices

The important issue here is often the cultural and environmental disruption that comes with moving offices within a firm. The assumption is often made that the culture, environment, values, ways of doing things and politics of another office will largely replicate those of the previous office, particularly in the case of moves from head office to a regional office or a local office abroad. This is often a very basic misconception, and can lead to a misguided attempt to replicate (and even impose on others) the culture and methods of the previous office. More often than not, this will cause resentment on both sides (ie, on the part of the new arrival and colleagues in the host office), and lead to the new arrival becoming isolated. Coaching can help the coachee explore the new environment, understand his or her place in it (and particularly how others perceive them), build a local support network and act their way into their new role and practice.

1.4 Career breaks

Returns from career breaks can often generate doubts and internal conflicts about work–life balance; a feeling that one is not competing on a level playing field; and issues around flexible working. Coaching for confidence, learning to sell oneself effectively, building a personal brand and role modelling are among the topics that come up most frequently in this context.

1.5 Moving firms

The major issues here are around understanding and adapting to the culture, values and methods of the new environment, building internal support and preserving and developing a book of business. For example, there is potentially a huge change in terms of cooperation and other areas, when moving from a lockstep to an eat what you kill environment. This may not suit someone who values collegiality above all things, but may well suit those with a strong taste for autonomy, politics and an entrepreneurial drive. The converse is true as well: moving from a highly autonomous and entrepreneurial environment to a lockstep firm can cause cultural problems and behavioural clashes. Coaching can help coachees explore, before making the decision to move, what their strengths, values and personal drivers are and whether the new environment will be a good fit for these. It can also enable coachees to assess the impact that the move will have on work–life balance. The ability to weigh these factors effectively will often get lost in the *sturm und drang* and excitement of a potential move, not least its financial attractions. Post-move, coaching can

"[T]here is potentially a huge change in terms of cooperation and other areas, when moving from a lockstep to an eat what you kill environment."

(as in the case of the move to a new office, discussed above) help coachees explore the new environment, understand their place in it (and particularly how others perceive them), build a local support network and act their way into their new role and practice.

1.6 Integrating new teams and mergers

The main challenges of integrating laterally hired teams or integrating them post-merger are fostering trust and collaboration, and avoiding tribalism. After the initial enthusiasm, resentment may build. This might be, for example, because of the perception that special deals have been done, or because of the new team's alien culture and methods, which may cut across conventions in the host firm. Political tensions and rivalries develop fast in these circumstances, and can undo the synergies and other benefits of the new hire or merger. Strong leadership and clear direction are essential, and team coaching can help considerably. See the discussion in chapter III, section 3, "Effective legal teams".

2. The stages in a lawyer's career

2.1 The four-dimensional lawyer

I find it helpful to look at a lawyer's personal development in four dimensions:

"As a lawyer progresses in seniority, he or she will need to expand their world view by learning to reach out and develop direct client contacts as well as political and professional support networks within the firm, beyond their immediate teams."

- Thinker: black letter lawyer, analyser and creative solution-finder;
- Doer: solution implementer, deal doer, negotiator and contentious lawyer;
- Developer: business getter and relationship builder; and
- Supporter: people developer, leader and team builder.

The environment and culture in which lawyers evolve play a big role in supporting the development of these four dimensions. In addition, contemporary evolution in attitudes plays a role: for example, the expectations of millennials entering the profession today are changing. They aspire to becoming doers and developers earlier in their careers and do not necessarily aspire to partnership. Work–life balance and learning are their priorities.

The following paragraphs focus on the typical career path of a lawyer in a large international firm, although most of what is said is equally applicable to legal careers in other contexts.

2.2 The trainee and junior lawyer

In terms of development goals, a good trainee and junior lawyer is expected to show more thinking and doing skills, but will also be expected to demonstrate the potential to become a developer and supporter.

Junior associates transitioning to senior associate status are often ignorant of, and unprepared for, the developer and supporter roles, and training can help considerably. The key trainable skill here is effective communication. Learning to listen, to conduct critical conversations and client networking conversations, to delegate well and take and give regular feedback are all key communication skills that underpin effective developer and supporter roles.

2.3 Senior associates and junior partners

Another important characteristic of a lawyer's development into senior associateship and through to partnership is the ability to reach out, engage proactively with others both inside and outside the firm and think ahead, both strategically and tactically. A lawyer will start his or her career receiving instructions, and be expected to execute them well. Their world at this stage is a small one: it generally consists of their immediate colleagues, particularly the senior associate(s) and partner(s) who give them most of their work. These will form their professional sphere. Their contemporaries will be their principal support network.

As a lawyer progresses in seniority, he or she will need to expand their world view by learning to reach out and develop direct client contacts as well as political and professional support networks within the firm, beyond their immediate teams. The time horizon of their world view will also need to broaden considerably: they will need to fix goals and visualise where they want to be and the role they want to play increasingly far ahead, and plan their actions accordingly by deciding the professional development actions they will need to take, the external and internal brand they will want to build, and the alliances they will need to form to those ends. That will require understanding their potential and place in the firm and in the market, how they are perceived by colleagues, the resources that they can leverage, and an ability and willingness to reach out to people, take control of their career and make things happen, as discussed earlier.

2.4 A word from the sponsor

An additional crucial element in the transition from senior associate to partner in particular (but also in the transition from fixed share or local partner to equity) is the need for a strong, politically connected sponsor to back the candidacy. Senior associates are often ignorant of this dimension. A discussion of support, network-building and profile-raising in preparation for the transition may well bring this issue to the table. Developer and supporter skills are important in this context. On this topic, see also chapter IV, section 4, "What does it take to make partner?".

"In terms of strategy, the areas where partners often fall down as leaders are clarity, transparency and communication."

2.5 Partnership, post-honeymoon

As a junior partner settles into a new role, things can become lonely. The dynamics of support start to change, as the partner becomes his or her sponsor's competitor, and the need to develop independent client relationships become greater. In addition, the need to develop and nurture one's own team and raise one's profile in the market become stark realities. These are factors that those with ambition and a growth mindset find energising, but for some they may pose a challenge, particularly in terms of confidence. And as one progresses as a partner, it can become more difficult to talk openly to other partners for fear of exposing vulnerability. In those circumstances, the safe environment for open discussion offered by coaching can prove extremely valuable. Partners can also use coaching to decide what new or substitute support they can build to replace their sponsor, and formulate a plan and the means to achieve it.

2.6 Ten years a partner

Ten years in, things might be less lonely, but existential issues can spoil the fun. At this stage, questions around "What next?" might arise, and there may be a need to renew one's energy by formulating a new plan and purpose. In addition, some may find themselves in the grip of the tensions of a mid-life crisis. All this can lead to drift, loss of confidence, and despondency. At this stage, the issues referred to earlier about not feeling able to open up to one's fellow partners for fear of admitting vulnerability come very much to the fore. Once again, the safe environment for discussion afforded by coaching, together with the opportunity of reassessing one's place in the partnership, and one's professional goals, make coaching invaluable for mid-career partners.

2.7 Leadership and management

To misquote Shakespeare, in law firms some are born leaders, some achieve positions of management, and some have leadership and management thrust upon them. Lawyers are not natural managers, and many lack leadership skills. And yet the majority of law firms put partners into leadership and management positions without giving them any formal training. Those who assume those positions are often rainmakers with proven doer and developer skills, but less well developed supporter skills. However, this is changing as more firms offer their leaders and managers leadership training, together with coaching.

One of the issues with partner managers in law firms is that they are seen as firsts among equals, and sometimes afforded little respect for their management roles. In times of change or crisis they have to implement difficult decisions involving fellow partners and often take heavy flak from others who cannot get their way. It is not a job for the fainthearted.

In terms of strategy, the areas where partners often fall down as leaders are clarity, transparency and communication. Lawyers, like most of us, want to know what plans our leaders have both for us and to make the team, department or firm great. Very often, partner managers are too preoccupied with how they are going to handle their targets or their own futures to formulate, communicate and implement bold strategies. What ideas they do have are often poorly communicated, or not at all, with the result that trust drains away at both partner and associate level, as everyone feels rudderless and undervalued. In those circumstances, coaching can be extremely helpful to clarify goals and strategy, raise awareness about others' perceptions and needs, and encourage good communication and leadership behaviour.

Clarity, transparency and communication of strategy – contrasting approaches

- *How not to lead:* The first example involves a practice head in a local office of a large firm. The profitability of the office had fallen considerably below the firm average and the practice in question was struggling to maintain market share. The practice leader was a poor communicator and mistrustful of others. If he had a vision and strategy, he never communicated it and failed to engage with anyone other than his protégés. Associate morale was low, principally because of lack of regular feedback about performance, and ignorance about strategy and goals. Enthusiasm and buy-in were non-existent. Apprehension and rumours about redundancies were rife. Associates would stay cloistered in their offices, behind closed doors. Several partners and associates left. When laterals were brought in with their teams, senior associates became resentful. This ultimately led to further defections. No leadership training or coaching was ever offered to the practice head or any members of his group.
- *How to engage through great communication:* The second example involves a specialist group practice head in a firm which had suffered from personality clashes and attrition in the past. The firm had recently introduced a leadership training and support programme for its group leaders. The practice head was offered coaching as part of the programme support and used it to work on leadership and communication skills. She developed clear goals about where she wanted to take the group in the following three years, and a strategy for getting there. She formulated the goals and strategy (which, incidentally, involved plans to bring in a lateral hire) in consultation with the partners and the senior associates in her team, listening to and taking their thinking into account, and

making it clear to all the associates that their efforts were integral to the group's success. As a result, her team became stakeholders in the group's future and she succeeded in creating real enthusiasm and buy-in for her vision. Moreover, thanks to the practice head's transparency and communication, the senior associates understood that bringing in a lateral was important to the group's future financial and reputational success and would strengthen the business case for their partnership chances, rather than blocking their career progression.

2.8 Pre-retirement

Partnerships, particularly those operating in the United Kingdom as opposed to the United States or continental Europe, tend to encourage retirement earlier than in other professions, the principal reason being to ensure that younger partners are afforded access to, and a fair share of, equity in their most productive years. This leaves a generation of partners in their mid-fifties contemplating what they are going to do next. This is unsettling for many who, having devoted several decades to the law, have very little idea of what to do next, or how to go about it. This can create an elephants' graveyard of partners who are despondent or hang on to their positions and clients.

Pre-retirement coaching programmes, which some firms are adopting, help dissipate the fear surrounding the idea of loss of status and identity. The programmes encourage and support partners to think beyond the anxiety of retirement itself to the possibilities that lie ahead. Formulating plans and beginning to road-test them while still in work build confidence and enthusiasm about moving on. This will help ease client handovers and possibly accelerate retirement for those who are simply hanging on for fear of letting go, as well as boosting morale in teams whose leaders are retiring. That can only be good for firms, and retiring partners, alike.

Many of the techniques for successful pre-retirement coaching are common to most types of transition and have been discussed in chapter V, "Coaching yourself and others through change", as well as the earlier paragraphs of the present chapter. However, a number of considerations are fairly specific to this situation. One of them is expectation management: senior retiring partners often have unrealistic expectations and aspirations about how their experience and former status will be perceived by the outside world. So if a coach can help the retiring coachee discover and develop a sense of what really matters to them, as well as patience, resilience and humility, that will help considerably. Other ideas relevant in this context may revolve around the confidence to experiment, the ability to listen, learn, let go, visualise possibilities, develop a personal narrative or 'brand', and motivation. And there may well be discussions around priorities, status, identity, self-worth, family, financial issues, using existing support and business networks, building new ones and identifying the community that will replace the working environment that is being left behind.

VII. Wellbeing

This section should really be at the beginning of this Special Report. Being aware of how you feel in mind and body, and taking the steps to ensure your personal wellbeing, are the foundation stones of self-leadership.

1. Energy budgets

Your time and energy are like a bank balance. After you have paid the bills, you're left with amounts that you can spend as you want.

Balancing the energy budget – the questions to ask

- Am I budgeting properly? How do I spend my daily 24 hours, and which parts of the day renew or call on my energy? Is that different from what I want? How can I make sure I get closer to my ideal budget?
- What am I doing to renew my energy? For example, am I sleeping enough, taking enough physical exercise and getting enough mental rest (see below)?
- Do I prioritise the use of my time and energy effectively? Do I gravitate instinctively towards things that are unimportant or not particularly urgent rather than tackling the urgent or important things?[27]
- What expenditure can I cut out? What things do I find draining and could do less of? For example, could I delegate more?

- Am I spending my time and energy on the right things? For example, am I spending the right amount on my family, social connections and support network? If I was to leave this firm tomorrow, where and with whom would I wish I had invested more time and energy?

2. Mindfulness and microbreaks

How can you avoid feeling overwhelmed when you have so much clamouring for your attention? People need to feel in control, so if they create small islands of time which are their own and in which they can be in the moment, they will feel less overwhelmed. Give yourself permission to do what you need first, and what others need second. Be disciplined here, and take those breaks: hold yourself or get a colleague to hold you to account, and make it a habit. It will be one of the most important habits in your life.

Lawyers are driven by time targets as much as by financial targets. Perversely, that is a built-in incentive not to spend time on yourself. Law firms should set personal debt time targets alongside billable hours, business development and firm contribution targets. In fact this is such an obvious suggestion that I'm sure many do, although this appears to be far from a widespread practice.

A great way to rest the mind and renew your energy during small breaks is by practising mindfulness. This is not a mysterious thing requiring years of apprenticeship to master. It is extraordinarily simple. The key ingredients of mindfulness are:

- regularity, as with physical exercise;
- breathing; and
- noticing one's thoughts, emotions and physical state.

For those who would like to find out more, there are many courses, apps, YouTube videos and books to guide you.[28] The regular practice of mindfulness brings different things to different people including:

- feeling calmer;
- sleeping better;
- noticing moods and emotions and accepting rather than fighting negative emotions;
- better breathing;
- perceiving things and people positively and less judgementally;
- greater patience, listening and empathy; and
- an improved ability to see things in perspective.

Before leaving this topic, I'd like to share one habit that I used to practice during times of stress. Every morning, fix on one thing that you can look forward to that day. It can be the tiniest thing. And be ruthless about making time and giving yourself the opportunity to enjoy it. Then, at the end of the day, remember one thing that you were happy with – again, it could be the tiniest thing – and be grateful for it.

3. Sleep, diet and exercise

Sleep, diet and exercise are often the first things that are sacrificed under time pressure and stress. Once a good sleep, diet or exercise pattern is broken, it is difficult to repair because it requires a great deal of precious mental energy in the form of discipline to do so.

It is far beyond the scope of this report, and outside my area expertise, to give advice in this area. However, I would recommend *Why We Sleep: The New Science of Sleep and Dreams* by Matthew Walker as a very readable and compelling analysis of sleep, its literally vital importance and how to maintain good sleep patterns.[29]

4. Fear and loathing in law firms – a plea for psychological safety

In the introduction to this Special Report, I wrote that while work–life balance, wellbeing and career choice were hardly new preoccupations when I was an associate and a partner, they were rarely addressed or

"In the competitive, Darwinian world of a high-performing business, you do not want to be the weak one in the herd."

even spoken about. This has now changed for the better in most law firms, although there is one thing that often remains taboo: talking openly about fear and vulnerability.

Most lawyers experience fear and psychological insecurity at one time or another, partly because all businesses work that way. Management will play on lawyers' hopes and fears to incentivise profitable behaviour, but that is of course only one cause. For many, fear and stress are a source of energy and drive, just as an arrow needs a taut bowstring to fly straight and true. But for many others, fear – of making a mistake, of not being recognised or respected, of being seen as underperforming, of being considered inadequate, of losing their job, and so on – is a paralysing affliction, and itself creates another fear: that of being perceived as vulnerable. In the competitive, Darwinian world of a high-performing business, you do not want to be the weak one in the herd. So admitting vulnerability, and asking for help, is not something we do easily even though outing that fear and sense of vulnerability is the key to dealing with and conquering it. Understanding that we all feel it, that many fellow lawyers are in the same situation, and that it is not a sign of inadequacy to talk about it, is an important step on the journey to put fear behind us, or at least own it and work through it.

I have witnessed the destructive effects of law firm environments where partners do not openly express their hopes, let alone their concerns about their positions and their future, and where fear and lack of psychological honesty engenders mistrust, the formation of cliques and tribes and, in some individual cases, loathing.

Good leadership – and good self-leadership – requires recognising insecurity in oneself and others and creating an environment where talking about it is considered acceptable and safe, particularly in times of change and adversity when fear takes hold easily. This is why building trust through good leadership is so important in law firms, as well as the many little things that contribute to that trust: gratitude, smiles, availability, open doors, appreciation, connection, floor-walking and open conversations.

Appendix 1: Self-appraisal

Table 3: SWOT analysis grid with questions

Strengths	Weaknesses
What do you do well? What unique resources can you draw on? What do others see as your strengths?	What could you improve? Where do you have fewer resources than others? What are others likely to see as weaknesses?
Opportunities	**Threats**
What opportunities are open to you? What trends could you take advantage of? How can you turn your strengths into opportunities?	What threats could harm you? What is your competition doing? What threats do your weaknesses expose you to?

Table 4: What kind of leader am I?

Core values/ beliefs	Drivers or guiding principles	How does that shape my leadership behaviour?	How do others perceive that behaviour?	What could I do more/less of?
Integrity	Be transparent with managers and subordinates.	I always deliver the bad news as well as the good. I share strategy and goals with my subordinates.	My superiors appreciate honesty. Only the mediocre leaders want yes men. My team derive a sense of buy-in and shared purpose from my readiness to share strategic thinking.	Take more credit for the good stuff! Learn to lead meetings so that everyone has their say and feels heard but I have the last word.
Courage	Never give up (if I want to succeed, double my failure rate).	I am bold and persistent. I do what I need to do to get ahead. I can say no. I have others' backs.	People see me as dogged (stubborn?) and ambitious. I've heard that some think I only take on assignments that suit me. My team are loyal because I will defend their interests in difficult times.	Learn when to let go and move on. Learn to sell my ambition better (eg, as a force for good in achieving sales targets). Appear less confrontational with managers when fighting my team's corner.
Respect	Do as you would be done by.	I always assume that everyone has something to bring to the party.	People say that I'm a good listener and that I'm good at gaining clients' trust by understanding their needs. Some members of my team take up too much time complaining to me about others.	Build on my listening skills (eg, through coaching?). Respect for people's feelings does not mean I should play the agony aunt. Use my courage and integrity to deliver tough love where necessary.

Appendix 2:
Partner/senior associate career planning template

This is a guide to thought, not a questionnaire. Not every question needs to be answered, nor every section completed.

The sample entries in the examples might be helpful. They are written from a partner's viewpoint, but they illustrate how a business plan might look like for senior associates as well.

Table 5: Where am I now?

Questions to consider	Examples/comments
As a person	
What are my strengths?	Useful strength-based self-assessments: Strengths profile StrengthsFinder Via survey
What do I enjoy doing most? What do I find rewarding, energising? What am I passionate about?	These are the things you might consider doing more of.
When do I feel at my best, most productive, most effective?	Ask colleagues and clients to give you examples of when you were at your best.
What values are important to me?	Values help to guide choices about work–life balance, personal priorities, type of practice and investment in non-client activities (eg, *pro bono*).
What do I find difficult, draining?	These are the things you might consider doing less of and delegating to others.
How would I describe myself in an honest paragraph (50 words max)? Which half-dozen adjectives/descriptive words would I use? Which words would others use?	Example: Colleagues say I'm authoritative, I put people at ease, I'm creative, a big-picture thinker, adaptable and solution-oriented. I believe I lack detail-focus and analysis; that I'm a good relationship builder but that I sometimes fail to follow through. Clients have said that I'm flexible and quickly grasp the business issues. I've had problems in the past with over-promising and under-delivering on deadlines and fees, which has adversely affected my relationship with some clients and associates.
Work–life balance	
How do I rate my work–life balance?	Factors might include professional vs personal fulfilment; family and social relationships, children; sport, hobbies, sense of wellbeing; stress; quality of sleep, exercise, diet.

continued on next page

Questions to consider	Examples/comments
As a professional	
How do I rate myself as a: Thinker (intellectual lawyer, analyser and solution-finder); Doer (solution implementer, deal doer and negotiator); Developer (business getter and relationship builder); and Supporter (people developer, leader and team builder)?	The Thinker/Doer/Developer/Supporter quartet is a helpful way of considering the facets of the "ideal" lawyer. Which are your strong facets, and which are development areas?
Practice focus and profile: What is my practice focus? What is my reputation/profile in the firm and in the market? How well am I known in the firm outside my office/region?	Do I consider myself, or do colleagues see me, as too much of a generalist or specialist? What does my Chambers entry say, or not say?
Resources: How would I rate the strength and quality of my resources? What is the size and shape of my team?	
Am I satisfied with my and my team's KPIs over the past 18 months in hours/utilisation; billing; and other?	What signals are my and my team's KPIs sending out?
Roles and responsibilities: What are my roles and responsibilities within the firm/practice group/office? Which sector groups and firm initiatives am I actively involved in? What non-client contributions do I make to the firm?	

continued on next page

Questions to consider	**Examples/comments**
Clients and network	
Client relationships: Who are my main clients? Which are key firm clients? How do I rate the quality and depth of my client relationships? Which individuals consider me (or potentially might consider me) as a trusted adviser?	
Connection: What is the strength and quality of my network within the firm? What is the strength and quality of my network outside the firm? Who is part of my support network? Who are my champions?	

Table 6: Where next?

Some questions
What is your vision for my practice? Where could you really make a difference in the market and in the firm in a way that plays to your strengths, enthusiasm and ambitions?
Where would you like to be in each of the goal areas below in the medium term (12–18 months) and in the longer term (3–5 years and beyond)? (You can set more than one goal for each area. This is not an exclusive list – feel free to adapt it to suit your case.)
Have you discussed your goals with the relevant people whose support you need, and have you got their buy-in? You'll need support to achieve your goals.
Have you had any feedback about any goal areas that you need to work on and take into account in your plan?
Are you aware of the firm/group/sector/regional/office plans that may be relevant to your goals?
Have you asked the partners you work for or with to share their business plans?
What conversations have you had with others to align your goals with theirs and create buy-in and support for your ambitions?
Some thoughts
Make each goal SMART (Specific, Measurable, Achievable, Realistic, Time-based).
The more specific and simpler the goal, the more likely it is to be successful.
Next steps in your action plan are commitments that you make to yourself and to others. Hold yourself to account by revisiting them every three months, preferably with a member of your support network and/or the persons whose support you have enlisted to achieve your goals.

Table 7: Goals and action plan template

Goal/ development area	Goals	Immediate next steps and action plan	By when?	With whose support?	How will I know I've succeeded?
Personal					
Work–life balance					
Practice focus/profile					
Practice focus					
Profile within the firm					
Market profile					
Skills					
Legal/ technical skills					
Matter management and organisation					
Commerciality and pricing					
BD and networks					
Business development and networking					
People					
People development and leadership skills					
Financials and firm					
KPIs					
Resources/team					
Roles and responsibilities in the firm, and other contributions to the firm					

Table 8: Goals template – clients

Client	Firm status of client	Client contacts	Development goals	How and with whom?	Success criteria
Client 1					
Client 2					
Client 3					
Client 4					

Table 9: Sample goals and action plan for refocusing practice

Goal/development area	Goals	Immediate next steps and action plan	
Practice focus: 12–18-month horizon	In the short to medium term I want to do less general banking work and more restructuring work for distressed debt investor clients, including X, Y and Z.	**Action 1:** Introduce [junior partner Seema] to clients A and B, who are the main sources of general banking work, with a view to Seema taking over some of that work. **Action 2:** Introduce one of my existing distressed hedge fund investor clients to [partners Ali in the London Restructuring group and Jurgen in Frankfurt] with a view to them introducing me to their London and German hedge fund clients. Arrange calls/meetings with Ali and Jurgen to discuss. **Action 3:** Arrange a marketing trip to present restructuring developments across several jurisdictions in one-to-one meetings with [name six hedge funds] in London, Frankfurt and [my jurisdiction]. **Action 4:** Attend firm's Restructuring Conference in Feb 2019. **Action 5:** Schedule 6-monthly follow-up discussions with [Jan, firm's worldwide head of Restructuring]. Diarise regular 3-monthly update discussions with [Leila, head of Finance for my jurisdiction].	
Practice focus: longer-term horizon	In the longer term I intend to become one of the top two or three go-to restructuring lawyers representing distressed debt hedge funds in [jurisdiction].	**Actions:** [List specific marketing and profile-raising activities, eg, joining an international restructuring industry group and speaking at one of their meetings, article-writing, marketing trips to London and NY to meet named clients etc.]	

	By when?	With whose support?	How will I know I've succeeded?
	Action 1: Arrange introductory meetings by end of Nov 2018. **Action 2:** Calls to Ali and Jurgen to discuss by 26 Oct. Make calls and send introductory emails to client by 16 Nov. **Action 3:** Calls to Ali and Jurgen to discuss trip by 26 Oct and finalise plan dates and presentation materials by mid-Dec 2018 with a view to marketing trip/meeting taking place mid-Jan 2019.	**Action 1:** Seema Leila, head of Finance for [jurisdiction] **Action 2:** London partner Ali Frankfurt partner Jurgen **Action 3:** Sundeep, head of Business Development for [jurisdiction] London partner Ali Frankfurt partner Jurgen Senior associate Dan **Action 4:** Jan, firm's worldwide head of Restructuring Jan's PA **Action 5:** Jan Leila My PA	I will know I have succeeded with this goal when the clients who are the main sources of my general banking work have started instructing Seema directly, and when I have received at least eight new instructions, enquiries, RFPs or referrals from distressed debt hedge fund clients, including but not limited to X, Y and Z, by the close of financial year.
	List deadlines for each action.	Leila, head of Finance for [jurisdiction] Jan, firm's worldwide head of Restructuring [Other relevant partners] [Relevant associates] Sundeep, head of Business Development for [jurisdiction] John, worldwide Restructuring Group Business Development Manager	I will know I have succeeded when I appear in the top Chambers ranking for Restructuring in [jurisdiction] with an entry that reads something like, "X is among the three go-to restructuring lawyers for mezzanine and junior distressed debt investors in [jurisdiction]. Clients have noted his ability to organise and negotiate effectively on behalf of large groups of creditors as well as his uncompromising and pragmatic solution-driven approach. He combines an understanding of the business needs and mindset of distressed debt investment funds with highly regarded local expertise."

Table 10: Sample client action plan

Client	Firm status of client	Client contacts	Development goals	
Sample client: Global Energy Industries Inc	Key global client	Rudi K, Deputy GC (MENA) Energy and Infrastructure Projects Hans M, Finance Director	**Goal 1:** Build a trusted adviser relationship with at least two board-level contacts. **Goal 2:** Become the firm client relationship partner for this client. **Goal 3:** Source instructions for MENA infrastructure projects worth USD X million in billings for 2018.	

	How and with whom?	Success criteria
	Goal 1: **By end-Nov 2017:** Arrange introduction to GC through Rudi; meet GC with [partners Y and Z, and the firm's Energy Sector Group head] to discuss new panel arrangements, secondment and cross-selling opportunities. **By end 2017:** Find out more about the finance director as an individual, and organise a marketing event (with GC also?) which plays to his tastes (FA Cup Final, Garsington Opera, West End Musical, West End movie premiere for his family?). Involve Sarah Z from London Projects BD for research and events organisation. Also involve firm's Project Finance Group head and firm's Energy Sector Group head. **Goal 2:** **By Feb 2018:** (Energy Sector Group offsite) – discuss possibility of co-leading the relationship at firm level with current client relationship partner, who will retire in 2019 (check date). **By Feb 2018:** Become more involved in Energy Sector Group. Arrange to speak at offsite. **Goal 3:** **By next March (panel renewal for this client):** Arrange to lead panel pitch, and ensure that we renew our place on the panel. As soon as possible, by end-Nov 2017 latest, discuss internally with management [specify who] possibility of putting favourable blended rate offer to client based on volume of infrastructure project work. **From next April:** Put myself forward as candidate for a partner secondment to work hand-in-hand with GC while his deputy is on maternity leave. Discuss plan with firm's head of finance, firm's Project Finance Group head and firm's Energy Sector Group head. Also liaise closely with and obtain buy-in from Julia F, the current client relationship partner.	**Goal 1:** When I have had at least three meetings and regular direct approaches for *ad hoc* advice from GC and FD in 2018 and beyond. When I am chosen to be the partner seconded to work with GC in 2018. **Goal 2:** When I am designated as firm relationship partner to succeed current relationship partner by mid-2019. **Goal 3:** **Step 1:** The firm renews panel place in 2018 with special volume-based fee arrangements guaranteeing increased share of wallet for infra projects. **Step 2:** Firm is actually instructed by this client on MENA infrastructure projects worth USD X million in billings for 2018.

Appendix 3:
Project management

Table 11: Sample tasks and responsibilities list

Workstream and task	Responsibility (individual)	Deadline
Workstream 1 – Corporate DD		
Corporate DD	Corporate Trainee 1/Corporate Trainee 2	02/03/18
Corporate DD report 1st draft	Corporate trainees & senior associate	04/03/18
Corporate DD report reviewed	Corporate senior associate	05/03/18
All DD reports integrated and DD report sent to client	Corporate partner & corporate senior associate	07/03/18
Workstream 2 – SPA		
SPA term sheet circulated internally	Corporate senior associate	03/03/18
SPA T/S internal comments produced	All workstream leaders	05/03/18
SPA T/S finalised and sent to client	Corporate partner & senior associate	06/03/18
Workstream 3 – Step plan		
Step plan 1st draft with corporate analysis circulated internally	Corporate partner & corporate senior associate	03/03/18
Step plan other workstream contributions	All workstream leaders	05/03/18
Step plan and transaction legal and tax analysis to client	Corporate partner & corporate senior associate	06/03/18
Workstream 4 – Finance		
Finance DD	Finance trainee	03/03/18
Finance DD report 1st draft	Finance trainee & associate	05/03/18
Finance DD report reviewed & sent to corporate	Finance partner & associate	06/03/18
Analysis of refinancing steps	Finance partner & associate	05/03/18

Table 12: Sample resourcing and scheduling Gantt chart

	04 March	05 March	06 March	07 March	08 March	09 March	10 March	11 March	12 March	13 March	14 March	15 March	16 March
Scheduling workstream 1: Corporate													
Task 1													
Task 2													
Task 3													
Task 4													
Task 5													
Task 6													
Task 7													
Task 8													
Task 9													
Workstream 2: Tax													
Task 1													
Task 2													
Task 3													
Task 4													
Task 5													
Task 6													
Task 7													
Resourcing workstream 1: Corporate													
Partner	Y	Y	Y	N	N	N	N	N	N	N	N	N	Y
5–7-yr associate	Y	Y	Y	N	N	Y	Y	Y	Y	Y	N	N	Y
1–3-yr associate	Y	Y	Y	N	N	Y	Y	Y	Y	Y	N	N	Y
Trainee	Y	Y	Y	N	N	Y	Y	Y	Y	Y	N	N	Y
Trainee	Y	Y	Y	N	N	Y	Y	Y	Y	Y	N	N	N

17 March	18 March	19 March	20 March	21 March	22 March	23 March	24 March	25 March	26 March	27 March	28 March	29 March
Double line marks end of Phase 1												
Y	Y	Y	Y	N	N	Y	Y	Y	Y	Y	N	N
Y	Y	Y	Y	N	N	Y	Y	Y	Y	Y	N	N
Y	Y	Y	Y	N	N	Y	Y	Y	Y	Y	N	N
Y	Y	Y	Y	N	N	Y	Y	Y	Y	Y	N	N
N	N	N	N	N	N	N	N	N	N	N	N	N

Phase 1 – number of days		
Y	N	CHk
7	9	16
12	4	16
12	4	16
12	4	16
8	8	16

Table 13: Sample costing and pricing spreadsheet

Phase 1 assumptions							
Standard utilisation: hours/day	6.5						
Discount	10%						
Rack rate margin	40%						
Workstream 1 – Corporate							
Costing	Rack rate	Discount	Time (days)	Time @ standard utilisation (hours)	Budget hours	Cost	Actual margin
Partner	£650	10%	7	6.5	45.5	£26,618	
5–7-yr associate	£350	10%	12	6.5	78	£24,570	
1–3-yr associate	£250	10%	12	6.5	78	£17,550	
Trainee	£170	10%	12	6.5	78	£11,934	
Trainee	£170	10%	8	6.5	52	£7,956	
						£88,628	30%
					External costs and disburse-ments	£12,000	
					Total	£100,628	
Workstream 2 – Tax							
Costing	Rack rate	Discount	Time (days)	Time @ standard utilisation (hours)	Budget hours	Cost	Actual margin
Partner 1	£500	10%	0	6.5	10	£4,500	
Partner 2	£500	10%	0	6.5	0	–	
5–7-yr associate	£350	10%	0	6.5	20	£6,300	
1–3-yr associate	£225	10%	0	6.5	0	–	
NQ	£200	10%	0	6.5	0	–	
Trainee	£170	10%	0	6.5	0	–	
						£10,800	30%
				External costs and disburse-ments	£7,400		
				Total	£18,200		
				Phase 1	Total	£118,828	

Notes

1 Sun Tzu, *The Art of War*, ed. and transl. John Minford (Penguin Classics, 2009), p4.
2 For those interested in the power of myths in the context of leadership, tribalism and history, I warmly recommend *Sapiens: A brief history of humankind* by Yuval Noah Harari (Vintage Publishing, 2015).
3 *Ibid*, pp 19, 68.
4 *Ibid*, pp 80–81.
5 Figure 1 and the five dysfunctions are reproduced by kind permission of The Table Group from the downloadable pdf available at: www.tablegroup.com/books/dysfunctions. See Patrick Lencione, *The Five Dysfunctions of a Team* (John Wiley & Sons, 2002).
6 Nancy Kline, *Time to Think: Listening to Ignite the Human Mind* (Cassell Illustrated, 2013).
7 Olivia Fox Cabane, *The Charisma Myth: Master the Art of Personal Magnetism* (Portfolio Penguin, 2013).
8 David H Maister, Charles Green and Robert Galford, *The Trusted Advisor* (Simon & Schuster UK, 2002).
9 Famous examples of former lawyers include Edwin Hubble, John Cleese and Henri Matisse.
10 www.strengthsprofile.com/en-gb/products/profiles.
11 www.gallupstrengthscenter.com/.
12 www.viacharacter.org/.
13 These career anchors were distilled out of longitudinal research conducted by MIT Professor Edgar Schein with Ivy League graduates over 40 years. For more on this and associated resources, see Edgar Schein's Career Anchors website at www.careeranchorsonline.com/SCA/startPage.do.
14 D Rock (2008). "SCARF: A brain-based model for collaborating with and influencing others", in *NeuroLeadership Journal* 1, 1994, pp44–52.
15 Albert Bandura, *Self-Efficacy: The Exercise of Control* (WH Freeman, 1997).
16 Mihaly Csikszentmihalyi, *Flow: The Psychology of Optimal Experience* (New York: Harper & Row, 1990).
17 For those who are interested in the neuroscience behind this, I recommend *Elastic: Flexible Thinking in a Constantly Changing World* by Leonard Mlodinow (Allen Lane, 2018).
18 Daniel H Pink, *Drive – The Surprising Truth About What Motivates Us* (Canongate Books, 2011).
19 E L Deci, "Effects of externally mediated rewards on intrinsic motivation", *Journal of Personality and Social Psychology* 18, 1971, pp105–115.
20 James O Prochaska and Carlo C DiClemente, "The transtheoretical approach", in John C Norcross and Marvin R Goldfried, *Handbook of Psychotherapy Integration*, Oxford series in clinical psychology (2nd ed.) (New York: Oxford University Press, 2005), pp147–171.
21 *The Hedgehog and the Fox: An Essay on Tolstoy's View of History* by Isaiah Berlin, W&N (2014).
22 See n 16 *supra*.
23 See, in particular, Daniel Goleman, *Emotional Intelligence and Working with Emotional Intelligence* (Bloomsbury, 2004).
24 J Luft and H Ingham, "The Johari window, a graphic model of interpersonal awareness", *Proceedings of the western training laboratory in group development* (Los Angeles: University of California, Los Angeles, 1995).
25 P R Clance & S A Imes, "The imposter phenomenon in high achieving women: Dynamics and therapeutic intervention", in *Psychology and Psychotherapy: Theory, Research & Practice*, 15(3), 1978, 241–247.
26 Carol Dweck, *Mindset: How you can fulfil your potential* (Robinson, 2012).
27 For more on this, I recommend *7 Habits of Highly Effective People* by Stephen R Covey (Free Press, 1989).
28 From personal experience, I would recommend the Oxford Mindfulness Centre courses (see oxfordmindfulness.org), Headspace and their online and app-based tools and resources (see headspace.com), and *A Mindfulness Guide for the Frazzled* by Ruby Wax (Penguin Life, 2016).
29 Matthew Walker, *Why We Sleep: The New Science of Sleep and Dreams* (Allen Lane, 2017).

About the author

Antonin Besse
antonin.besse@btinternet.com

Antonin Besse brings an insider's insights to the subject of leadership and self-leadership in law firms thanks to an impressive legal career – he spent over three decades as an international lawyer and 22 years as a partner with Freshfields Bruckhaus Deringer LLP, qualified and practising in both the UK and France – as well as his experience as a legal learning and development specialist and executive coach. His clients include leading law firms, financial institutions and public sector organisations. He works closely with Saïd Business School. He is also co-founder of Interview Advantage Ltd, which prepares undergraduates for the world of work. His other activities include cabinetmaking and understanding as much about cosmology and quantum physics as it is possible for a recovering lawyer to do. Antonin is French, and lives in Oxford.